# OUTDOOR MAKER LAB

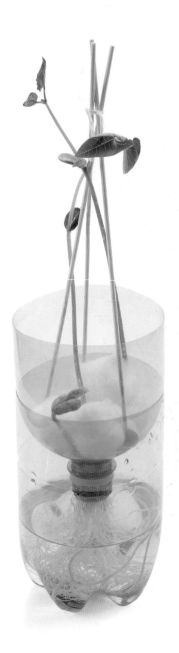

**Penguin Random House**

**Senior designer** Michelle Staples
**Lead editor** Amanda Wyatt
**Designers** Nicola Erdpresser, Sean Ross
**Illustrator** Edwood Burn

**Managing editor** Lisa Gillespie
**Managing art editor** Owen Peyton Jones
**Producer, pre-production** Andy Hilliard
**Senior producer** Alex Bell
**Jacket designers** Mark Cavanagh, Suhita Dharamjit, Juhi Sheth
**Jackets design development manager** Sophia MTT
**Managing jackets editor** Saloni Singh
**Jackets editorial coordinator** Priyanka Sharma
**Jackets editor** Claire Gell
**Jacket DTP designer** Rakesh Kumar
**Picture researcher** Laura Barwick

**Publisher** Andrew Macintyre
**Associate publishing director** Liz Wheeler
**Art director** Karen Self
**Publishing director** Jonathan Metcalf

**Writer and consultant** Jack Challoner
**Photographer** Dave King

First published in Great Britain in 2018
by Dorling Kindersley Limited
80 Strand, London, WC2R 0RL

Copyright © 2018 Dorling Kindersley Limited
A Penguin Random House Company
2 4 6 8 10 9 7 5 3 1
001–305992–March/2018

A CIP catalogue record for this book
is available from the British Library.
ISBN: 978-0-2413-0220-0

Printed in China

A WORLD OF IDEAS:
SEE ALL THERE IS TO KNOW

www.dk.com

# ROBERT WINSTON

# OUTDOOR MAKER LAB

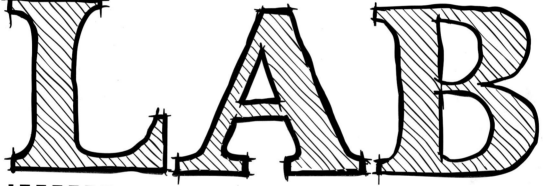

## EXCITING EXPERIMENTS FOR BUDDING SCIENTISTS

DK

# CONTENTS

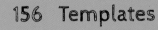

# FOREWORD

Whether it's a garden, a balcony, a park, or a forest, the outdoors is a great place to explore science and conduct experiments. The ones we've chosen for this book all look at the world around us, and doing them will help you understand more about nature and how science works.

There's so much to learn from the natural world, and this book is the perfect companion to those adventures. Many of the experiments are about water and how it moves and acts, some are about measuring and recording the weather, and others explore how plants grow and how animals behave.

All these activities and projects are a lot of fun, but it's important to be safe. None of the experiments are dangerous, but some of them will require an adult's help. Also, you shouldn't be afraid to make little changes, that's how scientists work in their research. Mishaps aren't setbacks. They are chances to learn more science, to tweak your approach and start again.

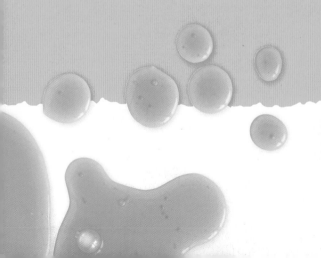

To get good results, you should do what all scientists like myself do: work with precision. That means taking great care in ruling straight lines, getting angles correct, and measuring things exactly. You'll also need to make sure that the numbers and lines on your builds are accurate. Measurement like this is at the heart of science because only by measuring things accurately can we work out how much something has changed, grown, or decreased.

I hope you really enjoy this book. It was doing practical stuff like this which made me want to become a scientist. I can tell you that I still find science as exciting as I did at seven years old when I did projects like these in the garden.

Robert Winston.

**ROBERT WINSTON**

# NATURE WATCH

Studying living things is a fascinating part of scientific study. In this chapter, you'll be growing plants without any soil and making your own recycled plant pots. You'll find out about animals, too, by making your own butterfly feeder, a home for earthworms, and even a periscope that will help you study other animals without them noticing you. You'll also be investigating fungi, by growing mycelium on cardboard.

Birds and animals often hide
if they spot a human. Your
periscope will allow you to
get closer without them
knowing you are there.

# PERISCOPE

Have you ever tried to watch birds or other wildlife without being seen? It's
hard to do! If you can *see* something, it can probably *see you* – and most
animals will stay away if they know you are there. That's why a periscope
is helpful. It lets you see round corners and peek over obstacles, which
means you can hide in long grass, or even behind a fallen tree, to watch
animals without disturbing them.

## BOUNCING LIGHT

There are two mirrors inside this periscope – one at the
top and one at the bottom. Each one changes the direction
of the light coming from the birds and other things you
are looking at. That's how you can see around corners, and
therefore *see* things without being *seen*. Your periscope is
perfect for using in the great outdoors, but take care not
to point it directly at the Sun.

Light enters the periscope through the opening here.

Your periscope is camouflaged — decorated in colours that allow it to blend into the surroundings.

# HOW TO BUILD A
# PERISCOPE

This project involves a lot of measuring and cutting, but if you take your time and be careful, you'll have a sturdy periscope you can use outdoors again and again. The paints are optional, but they'll help you stay camouflaged while you're out on location spying on birds or other animals.

**Time**
I hour plus drying time

**Difficulty**
Hard

## WHAT YOU NEED

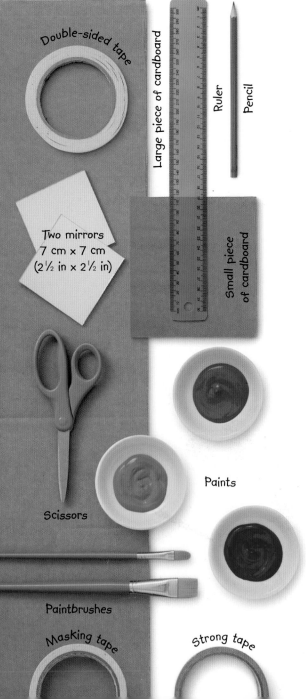

Double-sided tape

Large piece of cardboard

Ruler

Pencil

Two mirrors
7 cm × 7 cm
(2½ in × 2½ in)

Small piece of cardboard

Scissors

Paints

Paintbrushes

Masking tape

Strong tape

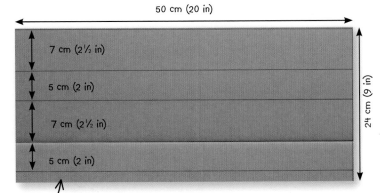

50 cm (20 in)

7 cm (2½ in)

5 cm (2 in)

7 cm (2½ in)

5 cm (2 in)

24 cm (9 in)

This narrow rectangle is 2 cm (¾ in) high.

1 Using the ruler, copy the design above, making each rectangle 50 cm (20 in) long. The narrow rectangle at the bottom will be a flap you'll use to stick the tube together.

These marks divide your periscope into three separate sections.

10 cm (4 in)

10 cm (4 in)

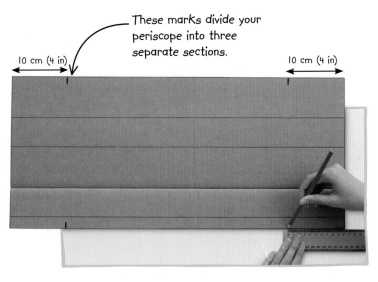

2 Make four guide marks, two on the top edge and two on the bottom edge of the shape you have drawn. They should be 10 cm (4 in) in from each end.

**3** Draw dotted lines as shown, connecting the marks you drew as guides, and using your ruler to make the lines straight. It's important to draw the dotted lines in the right place – an adult can help you.

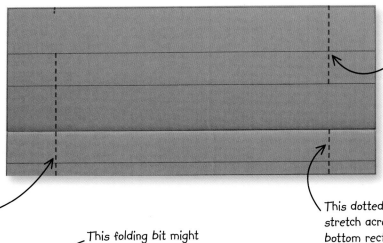

This dotted line should cover the two top rectangles only.

This dotted line covers only four of the five rectangles.

This dotted line should stretch across the two bottom rectangles.

This folding bit might be fiddly – ask an adult if you need help.

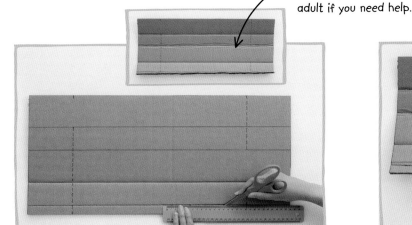

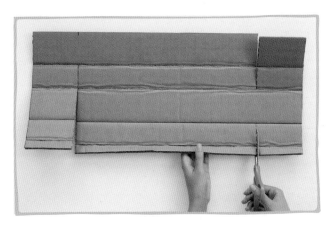

**4** Using the blade of your scissors and a ruler, carefully score along each of the horizontal lines. Fold along each score inwards.

**5** Cut along the dotted lines you drew. Make sure you don't cut all the way across the cardboard.

Unpeel the tape to reveal another sticky side.

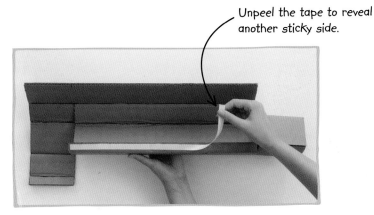

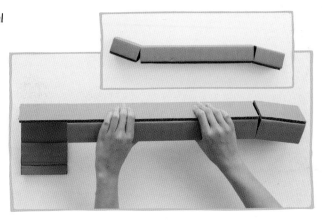

**6** Stick double-sided tape along the tabs at the bottom of each of the three sections. Unpeel the tape's protective strip.

**7** Now roll the tube together, and seal it by pressing down on the tab with double-sided tape.

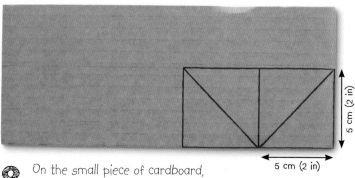

**8** On the small piece of cardboard, draw four right-angled triangles, with two sides measuring 5 cm (2 in) each.

5 cm (2 in)

5 cm (2 in)

**9** Carefully cut out your four right-angled triangles. These triangles will help to support the two mirrors inside your periscope.

Make sure that the tape covers any gaps in the sides of the periscope.

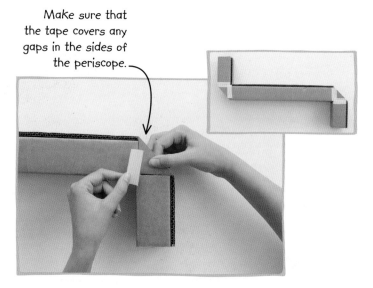

**10** With masking tape, stick the four triangles into the four empty gaps at each end of the periscope to create a square-shaped opening.

**11** At one opening, place the mirror with the reflective side pointing inwards. Repeat for the other end. The mirrors need to be at a 45° angle for the periscope to work.

Each mirror should now fit perfectly over the hole at each end of the tube.

**12** Use strong tape to fix the mirror to the tube. Do the same at the other end of the periscope.

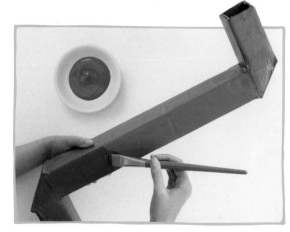

**13** Paint the periscope different shades of green and let it dry.

**14** You can improve the camouflage effect by cutting out some long, thin strips from any spare cardboard, and painting them green to look like grass.

**15** Stick small pieces of double-sided tape to the bottom of each blade of grass. Unpeel the protective strip and attach the grass to your periscope.

# HOW IT WORKS

When you *see* an object, it's because light coming from that object enters your eyes. Some objects, such as a computer screen, produce the light themselves, but most objects simply reflect light that has come from somewhere else, such as the Sun. Either way, the light coming from an object always travels in a straight line, so normally, you have to look straight at something to see it. But by arranging the mirrors inside the periscope in just the right way, you can guide the light that is coming from an object in a particular direction, so you can see an object without looking straight at it.

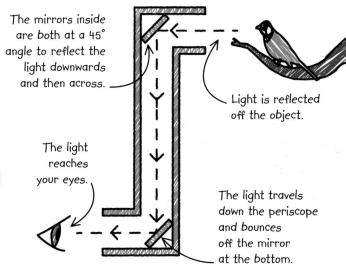

The mirrors inside are both at a 45° angle to reflect the light downwards and then across.

Light is reflected off the object.

The light reaches your eyes.

The light travels down the periscope and bounces off the mirror at the bottom.

# REAL WORLD SCIENCE
## UNDERWATER VISION

For a long time, periscopes were used on submarines so that the crew could see what was going on above the water's surface while they were submerged. These periscopes were more sophisticated than yours – they had lenses inside to provide magnification. Modern submarines have external cameras instead, which send pictures to screens inside the vessel.

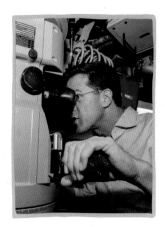

Hang this beautiful butterfly feeder somewhere high, such as from the branch of a tree.

## SUGARY TREATS

Try to find out what species of butterfly live in your part of the world. You could look in a book or search online to help you identify the butterflies that visit your feeder. Scientists think there are about 15,000 species of butterfly altogether, on every continent apart from Antarctica (the land around the South Pole).

Inside the cup there is orange juice.

# BUTTERFLY FEEDER

Like bees, butterflies are very important for plants. They pollinate flowers, enabling a plant to produce fruits and seeds. You can attract butterflies to your garden or balcony, or your favourite spot in a local park, with this simple-to-make butterfly feeder.

# HOW TO MAKE A
# BUTTERFLY FEEDER

To attract butterflies, your butterfly feeder needs to be bright and colourful, like a flower. Inside, you'll place a small piece of a flat kitchen sponge, soaked in sugary orange juice. Butterflies love the taste of the juice, so hang your feeder on a tree on a warm summer's day, and then watch and wait.

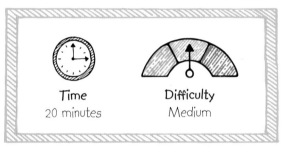

**Time**
20 minutes

**Difficulty**
Medium

## WHAT YOU NEED

String

Adhesive putty

Double-sided tape

Orange juice

Scissors

Pencil

Flat kitchen sponge

Paper cup

Plastic carrier bag

Be careful of the sharp pencil.

**1** Make two holes in opposite sides of the paper cup with the sharp end of the pencil. Use a lump of adhesive putty to protect the table.

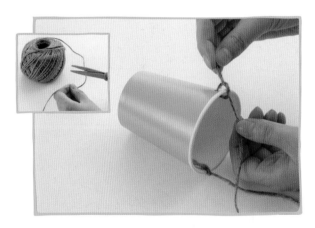

**2** Cut a length of string about 30–40 cm (12–15 in) long and push the ends through the holes in the cup. Tie the ends, so that the string makes a handle.

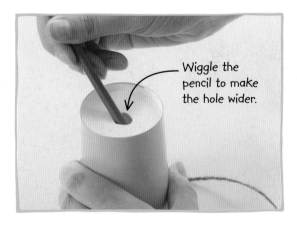

Wiggle the pencil to make the hole wider.

**3** Use the sharp end of the pencil to make a hole about 1 cm (½ in) in diameter, this time in the middle of the base of the cup.

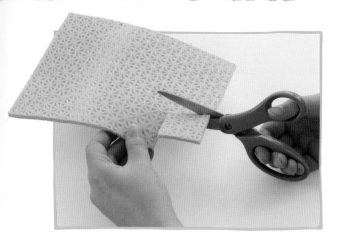

**4** Cut out a square with sides of about 2 cm (¾ in) from the flat kitchen sponge.

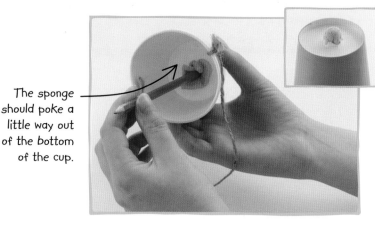

The sponge should poke a little way out of the bottom of the cup.

**5** Using the *blunt* end of the pencil this time, push the square of sponge into the hole in the bottom of the cup.

Cut out your flower into any design you like.

**6** Draw a flower onto the plastic bag and cut it out. Make your flower bigger than the cup's base, and cut a hole in the middle that is slightly bigger than the sponge poking through.

**7** Stick small pieces of double-sided tape to the base of the cup, and peel off the protective strips.

Press firmly to ensure your flower is securely attached.

**8** Press the flower down onto the base of the cup. Your butterfly feeder now just needs one crucial ingredient: orange juice.

The orange juice will soak into the sponge and slowly drip from it.

**9** Outside or over a sink, pour a little orange juice into the cup. Hang the feeder from a branch and watch hungry visitors flutter to it.

# TAKE IT FURTHER

Different species of butterfly may be attracted to different types of flower. Experiment with different coloured plastic bags, cutting them into any design you like, to see if certain butterflies are attracted to particular combinations. Try using different fruit juices, too – some varieties may be more popular with butterflies than others. Make notes of the visitors to your feeder to help you spot any patterns.

Try cutting your flowers into different shapes to attract different types of butterfly.

# HOW IT WORKS

The plastic flower shape is mostly for decoration, though it may help butterflies to notice the feeder. What they are after is the sweet orange juice dripping from the sponge at the centre of the flower. A butterfly's taste organs are on its feet. That way, it can tell if it has landed on a flower that is safe to eat. When the butterfly is satisfied it has landed on something tasty, it extends its "proboscis", a long, curled feeding tube that protrudes (sticks out) from the front of its head.

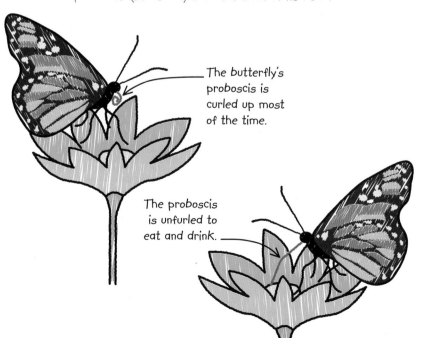

The butterfly's proboscis is curled up most of the time.

The proboscis is unfurled to eat and drink.

# REAL WORLD SCIENCE
## BUTTERFLY OFFSPRING

A butterfly tastes plants not just for itself, but also for its offspring: caterpillars. If the plant tastes good, the butterfly may lay its eggs there. Caterpillars hatch from the eggs and immediately begin chomping on the plant. A caterpillar spends its first few weeks eating and grows to many times its original size. Eventually it attaches itself to the plant and becomes a chrysalis. Several weeks later, the chrysalis becomes a butterfly.

These eggs have been laid on this leaf so the caterpillars can begin eating it when they hatch.

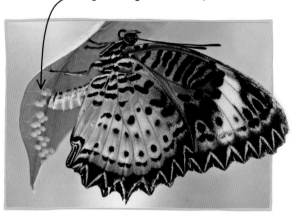

Your worms will burrow through layers of sand and soil.

It's important to keep the sand and soil moist because worms need water, just like you do.

# WORMERY

Despite having no bones, no legs, and no eyes, amazing earthworms work very hard. They churn up the soil, allowing air and water in, and they eat plant waste and enrich the soil with their droppings – they are the perfect team of recyclers. In this activity, you'll be making your very own wormery – a habitat for your worms to live in while you study them. Be sure to check it every day – you'll be surprised how quickly your worms get to work.

Since earthworms prefer darkness, your wormery needs a cover that will keep out the light.

## WORMING AROUND
Earthworms drag organic matter from the surface underground, and turn over the soil. They push themselves into the soil by creating wave movements in the muscles along the length of their bodies.

# HOW TO MAKE A
# WORMERY

You will need worms for this activity. If you have a garden, you might be lucky and find some there. They often come to the surface after it rains. If not, you can get them from pet shops, garden centres, or even on the Internet. Be gentle with them – they are living creatures. Worms are sensitive to light, so make sure you keep them out of the light as much as you can. When you've finished handling the soil and the worms, remember to wash your hands.

**Time**
30 minutes plus drying time for the paint

**Difficulty**
Medium

## WHAT YOU NEED

Paintbrush

Felt-tip pen

Scissors

Paints

Coloured tape

Sand

Soil

Dark-coloured A3 card

Large plastic bottle

Plant pot

Plant pot tray

**1** Start by decorating your plant pot. We've used green and yellow paint, but you can use any colours and designs you like.

Keep this card to use later.

**2** Wrap a piece of card around the bottle and, using the felt-tip pen, draw one line around the bottle near the top and another near the bottom.

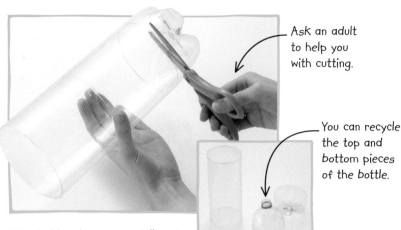

Ask an adult to help you with cutting.

You can recycle the top and bottom pieces of the bottle.

**3** With scissors, carefully cut along the lines you drew. You should now have a plastic cylinder that is open at both ends.

**4** Use the tape to cover up any rough edges of the cut ends of the plastic cylinder. Carefully wrap the tape all the way around and fold it over.

Fill the cylinder to within a few centimetres of the top.

**5** Stand your plastic cylinder in the decorated plant pot. Add some soil into the bottom of the pot and around the outside of the cylinder to secure it in place. Be careful to wash your hands after handling soil, grass, and leaves in this activity.

**6** Pour alternating layers of soil and sand into the cylinder. The soil layers should be thicker than the sand layers. Worms need water, so if the soil is very dry, make it damp by spraying on some water. The worms' home is nearly ready.

**7** Your worms will need some organic (living) matter to eat. Put some grass and leaves on top of your column of soil and sand.

Use wet hands to handle the worms, and don't squeeze them.

The worms will drag the grass and leaves down into the soil.

Use a short piece of tape to close up the cover at the top.

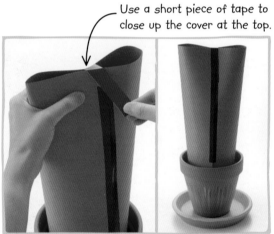

**8** Worms thrive in dark conditions. To encourage them to venture to the edges of the wormery, so you can see what they do, you need to make a cover. Wrap a piece of dark-coloured card around the cylinder and tape it securely in place.

**9** Now it's time to add the worms. Handle them carefully, with wet hands. Gently place about four or five worms on top of the grass, then slide the cover over the top. Wash your hands, then leave the wormery in a cool, dark place and check it each day. After a few days, return your worms to the great outdoors by tipping the wormery out into a flowerbed.

## TAKE IT FURTHER

You could make a larger wormery, in which earthworms can recycle kitchen waste, using a large plastic box. Keep it outside in a cool, dark place, and allow air in by making holes in the box or by leaving the top of the box open. Add vegetable peelings and egg shells, but no meat or fatty foods like cheese. You'll need to wait a while, but after a few weeks or months, the worms will have digested the kitchen waste and the box will be filled with rich, fertile compost that you can use in a plant pot or garden.

## HOW IT WORKS

It doesn't take long for the worms to get to work, churning the soil layers as they burrow. In just a few days, the soil will have been made richer by the solid waste that emerges from a worm's anus after it has eaten the soil. To help it slide through the soil, the surface of an earthworm's skin secretes (releases) a slimy liquid called mucus. Worms get rid of waste products (the equivalent of having a wee) through several pairs of tiny holes called nephridia that lie along their bodies.

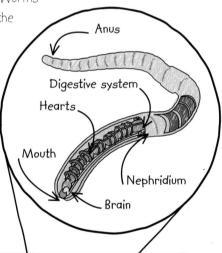

Anus
Digestive system
Hearts
Mouth
Nephridium
Brain

## REAL WORLD SCIENCE
### COMPOST

Many gardeners put earthworms to good use in their compost bins. Once the plant waste (vegetable peelings, dead leaves, or grass cuttings) is added, the worms drag it under the surface to eat. The worms then shred and partially digest the waste, mixing it with the soil. By adding worms to a compost bin, gardeners can increase the rate at which their plant waste becomes rich compost.

# EROSION BOTTLES

Soil is more than a place for plants to grow: it holds the nutrients and water that plants need. We depend on soil, too, because we need the plants that grow in it. Not only do plants produce the oxygen we breathe and the food we eat – we also use them to make shelter, clothes, and medicines. This experiment shows how unprotected soil can be washed away by rain, causing damage to the environment, and it also reveals how the plants dependent on soil to survive can help protect it.

The water has carried particles from the soil.

## CLOUDY OR CLEAR?

In this experiment, water running through bare soil erodes (takes away) some of the soil – that's why the cup on the left is cloudy. A layer of mulch (fallen leaves or other dead plant material) in the middle bottle protects the soil, and the water runs off less cloudy. But soil with plant roots anchoring it in place is the best protected, and the water running out of the soil is almost clear.

Soil is made of tiny pieces of broken rock, plus the remains of long-dead plants and animals.

The grass roots hold on to the soil.

The water is clear because very little soil has been washed away.

# HOW TO MAKE
# EROSION BOTTLES

This dramatic experiment is easy to do, but you will need to have some patience. Start setting it up at least a week in advance, to give the grass time to grow in one of the bottles. When you actually run the experiment, it's best to do so outside if you can.

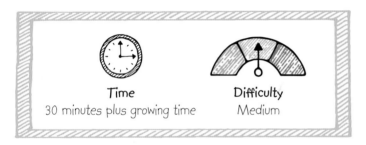

**Time**
30 minutes plus growing time

**Difficulty**
Medium

## WHAT YOU NEED

Three plastic cups

Felt tip pen

Pencil

String

Adhesive putty

Grass seeds

Scissors

Watering can

Mulch

Three large plastic bottles

Soil

Use a ruler if you find it hard to draw straight lines.

**1** Draw a large rectangle on one bottle with the felt tip pen. You need to make the hole big enough to put soil and then water into the bottle.

**2** Cut along your lines and remove the rectangle shape you drew from the bottle. An adult can help you. Recycle the piece of plastic you remove.

**3** Repeat the previous steps for the other two bottles, so you have three bottles just the same. Put two of the bottles to one side for now.

**4** Put a layer of soil a few centimetres deep into one of the bottles. The level of the soil should be just below the lid of the bottle.

**5** Sprinkle the grass seeds onto the soil, then wash your hands.

Don't add so much water that the soil becomes waterlogged.

**6** Using your watering can, pour water over the grass seeds. Use enough to make the soil damp.

**7** Leave the bottle in a place where it will get lots of sunlight, and where it won't get too cold. Add a little water each day to stop the soil drying out. After a week or so, your grass should have grown.

**8** Once the grass has grown, you can prepare your other two bottles. Add about the same amount of soil to them as you put in the first bottle.

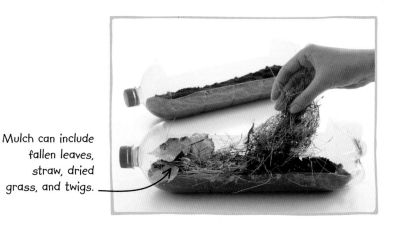

Mulch can include fallen leaves, straw, dried grass, and twigs.

**9** Leave one of the bottles with just soil. Into the other bottle, place a layer of mulch on top of the layer of soil. Now wash your hands.

Use a piece of
adhesive putty to
protect the table.

This bit is fiddly,
so you might
want to ask an
adult for help.

**10** Now you need to make three mini buckets. Near the top of each plastic cup, make two small holes opposite each other using the sharp end of the pencil. Put some adhesive putty underneath, before making the hole, to protect the table.

**11** Cut three lengths of string, each about 20 cm (8 in) long. Thread one end of a piece of string through one of the holes in the cup and tie a knot in it so it will not come back through. Then do the same in the hole on the other side, to make a handle.

**12** Make string handles for your other two cups. You should check that they are strong enough to hold the cups once they are full of water.

**13** Hang your buckets from the neck of your bottles. You are now ready to carry out the experiment. It might get messy, so be sure to do this part outside. Remove your bottle lids, then slowly pour water over each of the three bottles. The water will start to trickle through the soil into the buckets.

# HOW IT WORKS

Roots are crucial to a plant's survival. The roots grow down into the soil and absorb water into tubes that extend right up into the stem and leaves of the plant, above ground. Each grass plant has roots of many different sizes – from tiny fibrous roots up to bigger ones almost as big as the stem. The fibrous roots push out in all directions in the soil, not just downwards. The result is a complicated web of roots that holds the soil firmly in place. That's why the water runs out almost completely clear from the bottle with the grass growing in it.

When you have finished the experiment, lift the soil out of the grassy bottle by pulling on the grass. You'll see that the roots keep the soil in place.

You will be able to see hundreds of tiny roots twisting their way through the soil. It is these roots that prevent the soil from being eroded.

Try squeezing the grassy soil – you'll be surprised how much water is still in it.

# REAL WORLD SCIENCE
## SOIL EROSION

If it is left unprotected, soil can be swept away during heavy rains, taking with it the nutrients that plants need to grow. As this image taken from space shows, soil runs off into rivers and can be harmful to fish and other wildlife living there. Planting grass and trees along riverbanks can prevent soil erosion as they hold on to the soil, keeping rivers cleaner. Farmers can protect the soil they need for their crops and animals with a layer of mulch (dead leaves) or the roots of plants.

## FETCHING WATER

These bean seedlings have grown in damp cotton wool without any soil. As the plants grow, their roots reach downwards to find water. To become strong and healthy, the plants will need extra nutrients, but they can start to grow with access to only light and water.

The leaves reach upwards in search of light, which the plant needs to make food to help it grow.

The roots eventually grow down towards the water.

# SOIL-FREE PLANTER

How would you grow plants if you were on a long space mission, and your ship had no room for a garden? You'd use a technique called hydroponics, in which plants grow without any soil. Here, you can try it for yourself.

# HOW TO MAKE A
# SOIL-FREE PLANTER

This planter is easy to make, and it can be constructed mostly from simple household items. The bean seeds you plant will take a few days to germinate (begin sprouting roots and a shoot), and a week or two to grow into small plants.

**Time**
30 minutes plus growing time

**Difficulty**
Medium

## WHAT YOU NEED

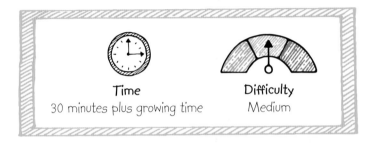
Modelling clay
String
Scissors
Bean seeds
Wooden skewers

Cotton wool balls
Large plastic bottle
Jug of water

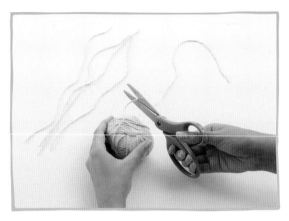

**1** Cut five pieces of string about as long as the bottle. Four will soak up water to feed the plants and one will tie the wooden skewers together to make a tripod to support the growing plants.

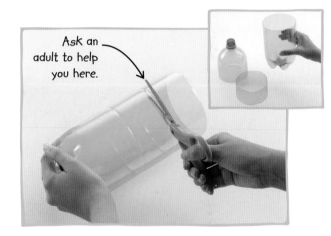
Ask an adult to help you here.

**2** Use the scissors carefully to cut a 5 cm (2 in) section from the middle of the bottle. Keep the top and bottom, and recycle the middle section.

**3** Place the top section upside down in the base section. This provides a platform for the seeds, and it stops the water evaporating.

Fill the planter with water up to this point, just below the neck.

The wet string will bring water to the growing seeds.

**4** Pour water into the planter so it fills the bottom almost up to the bottle's neck. The water should be about 10 cm (4 in) deep.

**5** Feed four of the pieces of string down through the opening of the bottle, but leave a few centimetres of each string in the top section.

Be careful of the skewer's pointed end.

**6** Put several cotton wool balls into the top of the planter, then drop a few bean seeds onto the cotton wool.

**7** To make a tripod that will support the stems of the plants as they grow, put a blob of modelling clay on the pointed end of each wooden skewer.

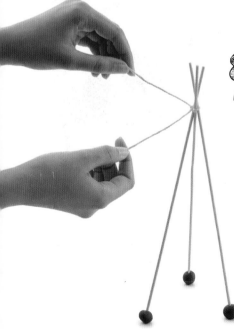

**8** Stand the three skewers on end and bring the tops together so they cross. Use the final piece of string to tie them together, to make a tripod.

**9** Place the tripod on top of the cotton wool, and put the planter in a bright place.

# HOW IT WORKS

Water from the bottom of the planter soaks up through the strings and wets the cotton wool. The seeds grow roots and a shoot when they absorb water. Water, air, and light are all a plant needs to start growing – that's why this plant can grow without any soil. A special chemical in the roots, called auxin, helps to direct them downwards so that they grow towards the water. Auxin makes a root grow more slowly on one side, causing it to bend in the direction of the force of gravity.

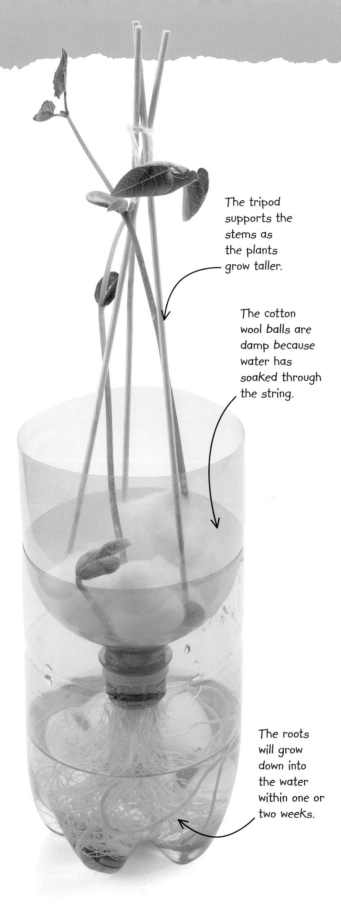

The tripod supports the stems as the plants grow taller.

The cotton wool balls are damp because water has soaked through the string.

The roots will grow down into the water within one or two weeks.

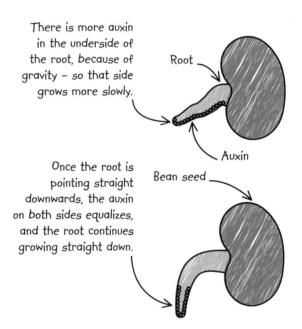

There is more auxin in the underside of the root, because of gravity – so that side grows more slowly.

Root

Auxin

Once the root is pointing straight downwards, the auxin on both sides equalizes, and the root continues growing straight down.

Bean seed

**10** The seeds should germinate after a few days. After a few weeks, transfer your plants to a pot with soil, or ask an adult to add fertilizer to the water, so the plants can flourish.

## REAL WORLD SCIENCE
## AQUAPONICS

Some plants are grown in hydroponic tanks, where they are fed water containing the nutrients, normally found in soil, that they need to grow quickly and healthily. Aquaponics, a type of hydroponics, feeds plants with nutrients from the waste products of fish kept in tanks. The fish provide food for the plants, and the plants filter the water for the fish.

# SEEDLING POTS

Gardeners use seedling pots to grow and protect young seeds. These homemade seedling pots are made with a torn paper mush, which is shaped around a plastic plant pot. Once the paper has dried out, plant a pea seed in the pot and watch it grow!

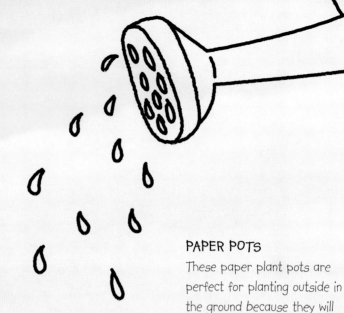

## PAPER POTS

These paper plant pots are perfect for planting outside in the ground because they will decompose (break down) in the soil without causing any harm.

These paper pots will break down harmlessly in the soil.

Each paper pot keeps the colour of the paper from which it's made.

# HOW TO MAKE
# SEEDLING POTS

In this activity, you make old paper into a wet mush called pulp, shape it into pots, and then let it dry. We've used sugar paper, but you could use any type of paper, including old newspapers. The paper pots keep their shape once they have dried out, and break down harmlessly once they have been planted in the ground.

**Time**
30 minutes
plus 24 hours drying

**Difficulty**
Medium

## WHAT YOU NEED

½ cup of flour

Soil

Jug of water

Plastic plant pot

Pea seeds

Glass bowl

Watering can

Two A3 pieces of sugar paper

Plate

**1** Tear the two pieces of sugar paper into strips about 1 cm (½ in) wide, and then rip these strips into small squares and put them in the bowl.

**2** Add enough water to the bowl to soak the paper squares. Don't add too much – just enough to make the paper very wet.

You could try adding more or less flour to your pulp to see how it affects your pots.

3 Pick up a clump of soggy paper and squeeze and scrunch it with your hands. Do this repeatedly until the paper feels like a mushy pulp.

4 Add the flour to your pulp and mix it in. Squeeze and stir the flour and pulp with your hands until they are fully mixed together.

Paper is made from cellulose, a strong, fibrous material found inside plants.

5 Take a clump of pulp and gently squeeze it to drain the excess water. Press it onto the side and the bottom of the plastic plant pot. Once you have covered the pot completely, stand it upside down, somewhere warm and dry for at least 24 hours, so it dries out.

6 When your paper pot is completely dry, you need to remove the plastic plant pot. Carefully loosen the paper around the top of the pot, then pinch the sides of the plastic pot together. Gently wiggle the plastic pot free from the paper pot.

Be careful not to crack the pot.

This step is tricky, so ask an adult to help you.

**7** Fill your pot with soil and plant the seeds about 1 cm (½ in) deep. Wash your hands after handling soil. Place the pot on a tray, in case any water seeps through, and leave it on a window sill.

Make the soil damp, but not soaking wet.

**8** Water the soil. Check your seeds regularly, adding more water if the soil is dry. Once the plants have grown to around 15 cm (6 in) tall, dig a hole and place the pot in the soil outside where it can continue to grow.

# HOW IT WORKS

A piece of paper is formed of millions of microscopic fibres, which are made of a material called cellulose. These cellulose fibres are tiny tubes that form the outer part (the cell wall) of plant cells. The cellulose fibres are linked together by tiny fibres called fibrils, but when you add water to the paper to make a pulp, the fibrils detach from the cellulose fibres. As the pulp dries, the fibrils rejoin, attaching the cellulose fibres together again. When you bury your paper pot in the soil, tiny living things (microorganisms) break down the cellulose fibres into smaller particles, and the paper gradually becomes part of the soil.

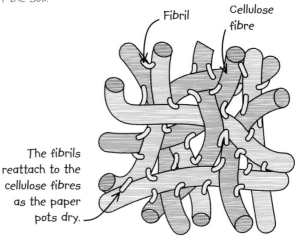

Fibril

Cellulose fibre

The fibrils reattach to the cellulose fibres as the paper pots dry.

## REAL WORLD SCIENCE
## PAPER RECYCLING

Paper is one of the easiest materials to recycle because the cellulose fibres it is made from can be mashed into a pulp and reformed into paper again and again. Recycling collections are taken to recycling plants, like the one in this picture, where the paper is separated into types, such as cardboard or newspaper, then cleaned and pulped.

# MYCELIUM

This mass of white fibres is called mycelium, and it is the main body of a fungus. Mycelium grows from reproductive cells called spores, which are released by another part of the fungus – its mushrooms. In this experiment, you will make mycelium in controlled conditions.

DO NOT eat the mushrooms or mycelium at any stage of this activity!

Oxygen, which the fungus needs to survive, enters the jar through a tissue paper top.

You will be able to see mycelium growing through the side of your glass jar.

### FEEDING TIME
Fungi don't make their own food, like plants do. They need to feed on something to gain energy and materials in order to grow. The mushroom spores that make the mycelium in this activity feed on corrugated cardboard.

# HOW TO GROW
# MYCELIUM

To grow a jar full of mycelium, ensure that your hands, the jar, and the cardboard are clean. If bacteria get into the jar, they may grow and compete with the mycelium. When you have finished this activity, ask an adult to throw away the jar's contents, and recycle the glass.

| Time | Difficulty | Warning |
| --- | --- | --- |
| 90 minutes | Medium | If you are allergic to mushrooms, don't do this activity. |

## WHAT YOU NEED

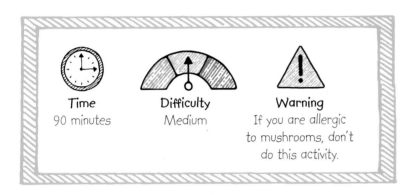

Jug of water

Microwave-safe lunch box

Scissors

Oyster mushrooms

Pencil

Rubber band

Clean glass jar

Corrugated cardboard

Tissue paper

You will also need a microwave oven

1 Draw six circles on the cardboard with the pencil. Trace around the bottom of the glass jar to ensure the circles are the right size.

2 Using the scissors, carefully cut out the circles. They will provide the surface on which the mycelium will grow.

Make sure the water completely covers the cardboard.

3 Place the cardboard circles in the microwave-safe lunch box and cover them with water.

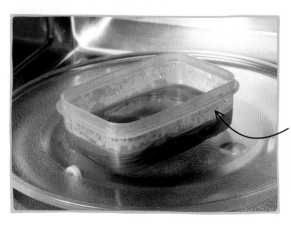

Heating the water kills any bacteria that might affect how the mycelium will grow.

**4** Put the lunch box in a microwave, and heat it on full power for two minutes without the lid. Let it cool down for an hour with the door closed.

**5** Before you remove the lunch box from the microwave, wash your hands thoroughly with soap, rinse them, and dry them on a clean towel.

You can get oyster mushrooms from any big supermarket.

**6** Lift the cardboard circles out of the water and squeeze them in your hand. This will get rid of some of the water they contain, but they should still be damp. Put them all on a clean plate.

**7** Place one cardboard circle into the bottom of the clean glass jar. Snip small pieces of oyster mushroom over the jar, making sure the pieces all land on the cardboard.

Ideally, the mushroom pieces will be near the middle of each circle, but don't worry about this too much.

**9** Add the damp cardboard circles one by one, dropping a few small pieces of mushroom onto each layer. Wash your hands after touching the mushrooms.

**8** Once you have a few pieces of mushroom on the first cardboard circle, add another damp circle on top and repeat.

The tissue paper allows in air, which contains the oxygen the fungus needs to survive.

**10** Don't put the lid on the jar. Instead, place a piece of tissue paper over the opening and secure it with the rubber band.

**11** Place the jar in a cool, dark place, such as a cupboard. Check the jar every couple of days. You'll be amazed at how fast it fills up with mycelium!

# HOW IT WORKS

A mushroom you *see* above ground is just a tiny part of a fungus. Hidden underground, beneath the mushroom, is a vast network of tiny threads that together make up mycelium. Fungi usually live in soil, rotting wood, or dead animals – anything that contains decaying organic matter. To reproduce, strands of the mycelium emerge from the soil, bunching into a knot, and grow into a mushroom. This mushroom then releases millions of spores, which scatter to make new mycelium networks.

If you have access to a microscope, you could use it to see if you can see the structure of the mycelium.

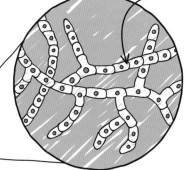

Mycelium is made of tiny threads, one cell thick, called hyphae.

## REAL WORLD SCIENCE
## MUSHROOMS

Some mushrooms contain nutrients that are good for us to eat, but many contain poisons, so don't eat any wild mushrooms unless an adult is sure they are safe. Mushrooms that are safe to eat are grown on mushroom farms, where farmers ensure that the humidity levels and temperature are kept as consistent as possible. Mushrooms grow best when they are kept in cool, dark, moist, and humid environments.

# WORLD OF WEATHER

The science of weather is called meteorology, and scientists who study it are called meteorologists. In this chapter, you'll be building four different meteorological instruments: a thermometer (to measure temperature), an anemometer (to measure wind speed), a barometer (to measure atmospheric pressure), and a rain gauge (to measure rainfall). You'll also investigate freeze-thaw action, and learn about how water and ice can cause erosion.

# BRILLIANT BAROMETER

It may be hard to believe, but the air around you is pressing on you from every direction! This powerful push is called atmospheric pressure, and it's measured using a device called a barometer. Weather forecasters use barometers to help predict how the weather will change over the next few days, as the atmospheric pressure changes.

## ATMOSPHERIC PRESSURE
Around Earth, there is a layer of gas more than 60 miles (100 km) thick – the atmosphere. The amount of air above you causes atmospheric pressure. This pressure changes all the time as air warms or cools, picks up water that evaporates, or loses water when it rains.

Record the straw's position on the scale every day. You will soon start to observe trends, and can then predict when those things will happen again.

The straw indicates changes in atmospheric pressure by moving up or down.

# HOW TO MAKE A
# BRILLIANT BAROMETER

This barometer is easy to make – you simply stretch a piece of rubber cut from a balloon over the opening of a glass jar. As atmospheric pressure increases, it pushes the rubber down against the air trapped inside, and as the pressure goes down, the rubber relaxes. Tape a straw to the rubber and watch it rise and fall as the pressure changes.

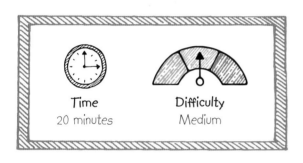

| Time | Difficulty |
|------|------------|
| 20 minutes | Medium |

## WHAT YOU NEED

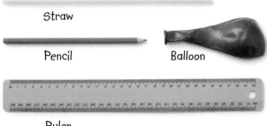

Straw

Pencil

Balloon

Ruler

Coloured card

Coloured tape

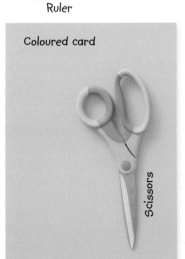

Rubber band

Scissors

Glass jar

1 Cut the neck off the balloon and throw it away immediately. This will make it possible to stretch the rubber over the jar's opening. There's no need to blow up the balloon.

Make sure you have a smooth surface.

2 Stretch the rubber over the top of the jar, trapping the air inside. Pull the rubber tight, to get rid of any creases.

3 Secure the rubber in place with an elastic band. No air should be able to escape the jar.

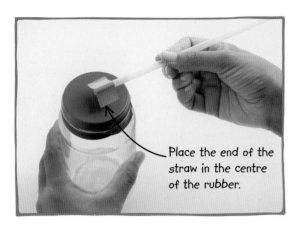

Place the end of the straw in the centre of the rubber.

**4** Cut a short piece of tape and stick it to the end of the straw. Now place the end of the straw across the middle of the rubber and attach it firmly.

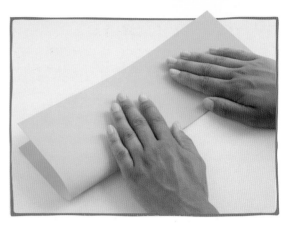

**5** To make the scale, neatly fold the piece of coloured card in half lengthways.

**6** Using a ruler, draw lines 1 cm (½ in) apart across one side of the folded card.

**7** Leave the barometer somewhere where the temperature doesn't change much, away from windows or heaters. If the air in the jar warms up or cools down it expands or shrinks, which will affect your results. Record the barometer's readings daily. Soon you'll be making your own weather forecasts.

The straw will be level at first, but over time it will move up or down.

When the straw is level, it indicates that the pressure inside the jar is equal to the pressure outside.

# HOW IT WORKS

If you press down on the rubber, you compress (squash) the air inside the jar. The air pushes back, so when you let go the rubber returns to its original position. The same happens when atmospheric pressure changes. When atmospheric pressure increases – when the weather is fine – the outside air pushes down on the rubber. Atmospheric pressure falls when rainy, unsettled weather approaches.

## LOW PRESSURE: RAINY WEATHER

When the atmospheric pressure is low, the weather is cloudy and rainy.

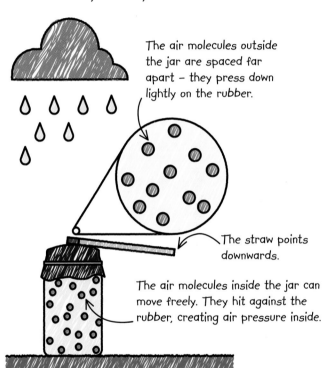

The air molecules outside the jar are spaced far apart – they press down lightly on the rubber.

The straw points downwards.

The air molecules inside the jar can move freely. They hit against the rubber, creating air pressure inside.

## HIGH PRESSURE: SUNNY WEATHER

High pressure means dry weather and clear, sunny skies.

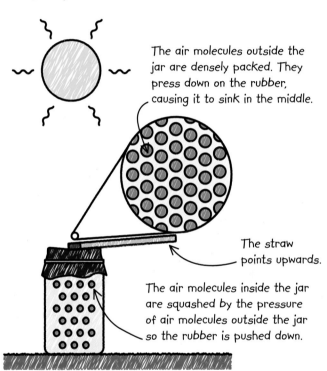

The air molecules outside the jar are densely packed. They press down on the rubber, causing it to sink in the middle.

The straw points upwards.

The air molecules inside the jar are squashed by the pressure of air molecules outside the jar so the rubber is pushed down.

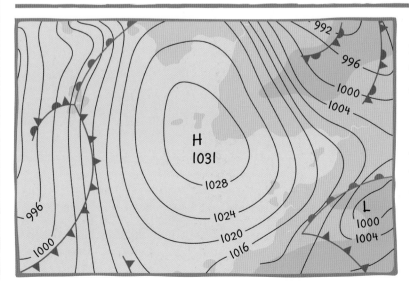

## REAL WORLD SCIENCE
### ISOBARS

You might have noticed that the maps used by weather forecasters on television are covered in numbers and wiggly lines. These lines are called isobars and they join up locations with equal atmospheric pressure. The higher the number on the bar, the higher the pressure. In areas of low pressure, storms start to form.

# RAIN GAUGE

Meteorologists, or weather forecasters, measure and compare rainfall over time to find patterns in the weather. With the help of weekly, monthly, and yearly records, they can predict when there might be heavy rain, or if a drought is on the way – vital information for farmers and gardeners. To measure rainfall, meteorologists use a device called a rain gauge.

Rain falls into the opening at the top of your rain gauge.

The rain gauge has a ruler stuck to the side, so you can easily measure how much rain has fallen.

### RAINY DAY
Do you live in a place where it rains often? Or is it very dry where you live? Does it rain more in the winter months or during the summer? Keep weekly, monthly, or even yearly, records of rainfall with your rain gauge, and find out!

# HOW TO MAKE A
# RAIN GAUGE

To make this simple rain gauge, you need to cut off the top of a bottle and make a flat surface at the bottom, inside the bottle, by adding gravel and modelling clay. There's a ruler stuck with tape to the side of the rain gauge that will allow you to measure and record how much rain falls in your local area.

**1** Wrap the card around the bottle, to help you draw straight. Draw a straight line around the bottle, about 10 cm (4 in) down from the top.

| | |
|---|---|
| **Time** 30 minutes | **Difficulty** Medium |

## WHAT YOU NEED

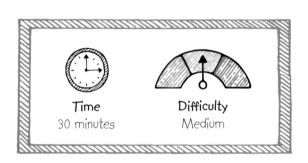

Scissors

Felt-tip pen

Coloured tape

Gravel

Ruler

Modelling clay

Coloured card

Large plastic bottle

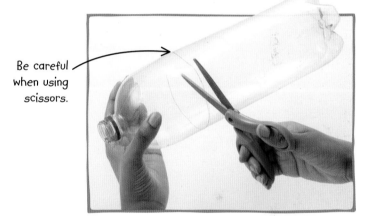

Be careful when using scissors.

**2** Carefully cut along the line to separate the bottle into two parts. Be careful of any sharp edges and ask an adult to help you if you're finding it tricky.

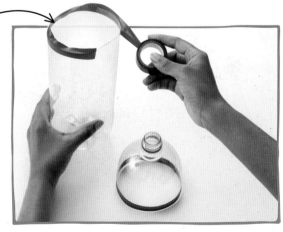

Fold the tape over here.

**3** Wrap tape neatly around the cut edges of the two parts, leaving enough to fold over. This will cover up any uneven cutting.

If your bottle has an uneven bottom, the layer of gravel will help to flatten it.

**4** Pour gravel into the bottom part of the bottle, to weigh down your rain gauge so it won't fall over.

**5** Press and mould the modelling clay into a thick, flat disc with the same diameter as the bottle. Make it as flat and smooth as you can.

**6** Push the modelling clay disc down onto the surface of the gravel and press it against the sides of the bottle, to make a watertight seal.

**7** Attach the ruler to the outside of the bottle with tape. Make sure the zero at the end of the ruler lines up with the top of the modelling clay disc.

The funnel covers the container, preventing the collected rainwater from evaporating (turning into vapour).

**8** Put the funnel upside down in the bottom part. Place your rain gauge outside, away from buildings or trees. After the next shower, go outside to check the water level and make a note of how much rain has fallen.

## TAKE IT FURTHER

Why not keep a diary of the rainfall over a year? If you empty out the rainwater from your gauge every week at the same time of day, you will have a set of weekly totals for the year. You could make a bar graph of your weekly totals to work out which are the wettest months – or you could compare your results with the average rainfall for other parts of the world, which you can find online.

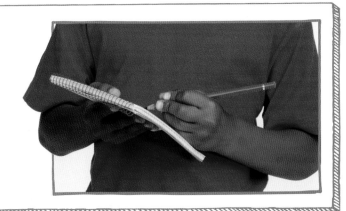

## HOW IT WORKS

When rain falls, it normally runs away down drains, or it soaks into the soil. If rain couldn't run away like this, it would collect on the ground, and the more rain that fell, the deeper the water would be. That's the principle behind a rain gauge: you are collecting rainwater that falls on a particular area – in this case, the circular opening at the top of your gauge – to see how deep the water becomes. If you made a rain gauge with an opening twice the size, it would collect twice as much water, but the depth of water collected would still be the same because the area of the bottom part of the rain gauge would have doubled too. If you had a rain gauge the size of a football pitch, it would collect thousands of litres of water in a single rain shower, but the water would still be just a few millimetres deep.

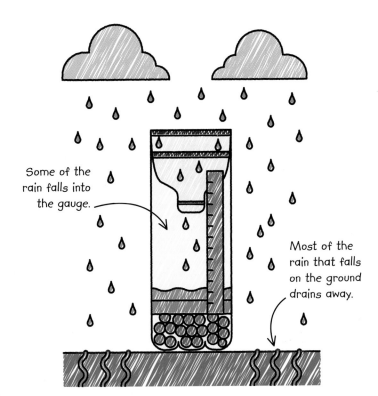

Some of the rain falls into the gauge.

Most of the rain that falls on the ground drains away.

## REAL WORLD SCIENCE
### WEATHER WATCHERS

Rain gauges are a very important piece of equipment for meteorologists and other scientists. They use the information they gather not only to keep track of how the weather in different places is changing over time, but also to predict what the weather is going to be like in the future. This can warn people about possible floods and droughts, and it also helps us to understand climate change. However, it's not just scientists that benefit from rain gauges. Farmers often use them to keep track of how much rain their crops are getting.

# THERMOMETER

A thermometer measures temperature (how hot or cold something is). There are lots of different types, but one of the most common is the liquid thermometer, a tube in which a liquid rises and falls as the temperature changes. These steps show you how to make a simple liquid thermometer that works inside and outside.

**HOT OR COLD?**
Try placing your thermometer in different parts of your home or outside space that are warm or cool, and watch as the water level in the straw goes up and down. You'll need to be patient: it will take a little time before the level of the water changes.

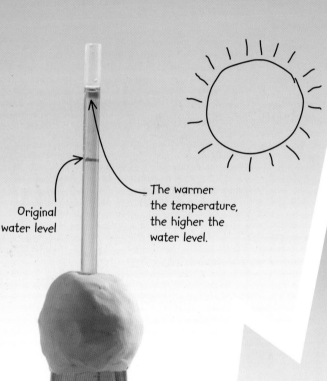

Original water level

The warmer the temperature, the higher the water level.

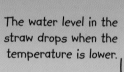

The water level in the straw drops when the temperature is lower.

Original water level

Food colouring is dissolved in the water, making it easier to see.

# HOW TO BUILD A
# THERMOMETER

It's easy to make your own thermometer, using coloured water as the liquid and a plastic straw as the tube. Once you've made your thermometer and tested that it's working well, you can create a temperature scale, in a process called "calibration".

**1** Fill the bottle with water almost to the top and add a few drops of food colouring.

| | | |
|---|---|---|
| ⏰ | 🌡️ | ⚠️ |
| **Time** | **Difficulty** | **Warning** |
| 30 minutes | Medium | An adult is vital as this experiment uses hot water. |

## WHAT YOU NEED

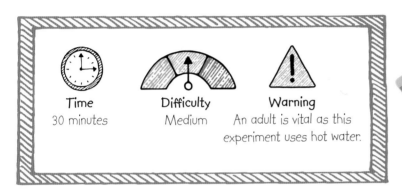

Modelling clay

Cooking oil

Food colouring

Clear plastic straw

Pipette

Felt-tip pen

Small bottle

Ruler

Glass bowl

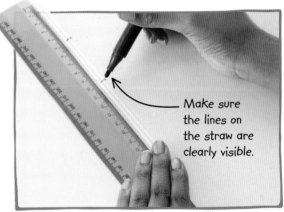

Make sure the lines on the straw are clearly visible.

**2** Mark your straw with two lines, one 5 cm (2 in) from the end and one 10 cm (4 in) from the same end.

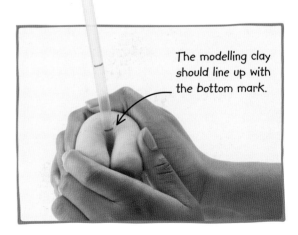

The modelling clay should line up with the bottom mark.

**3** Roll the modelling clay into a sausage shape and wrap it around the straw, so that the top of it is level with the bottom line.

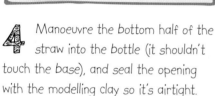

If the straw is too long, simply cut off a bit at the bottom end.

Add water into the straw until it reaches the top line.

The oil sits on top of the water because they are "immiscible" – they don't mix.

**4** Manoeuvre the bottom half of the straw into the bottle (it shouldn't touch the base), and seal the opening with the modelling clay so it's airtight.

**5** Mix more water and food dye, and use the pipette to add a few more drops of coloured water into the straw.

**6** Add just a drop of oil to stop the water evaporating (turning into vapour).

At higher temperatures, the water level in the straw rises.

Be careful not to spill any hot water or scald yourself.

The lower the temperature, the lower the water level falls.

**8** Now put cold water into the bowl and see what happens.

You could add ice cubes into the bowl to make the water really cold.

**7** Your thermometer is complete and ready to use. To test that it's working, carefully place it in a bowl of hot water. The water level in the straw should rise.

# TAKE IT FURTHER

The thermometer you've made only shows whether the temperature is high or low, but creating a scale by referring to a bought thermometer will give you more accurate temperature readings. This process is called "calibration". Start with hot water in the bowl and let it cool. Every so often, mark on your scale the water level and the temperature shown on the bought thermometer. To add lower temperature readings to your scale, put cold water into the bowl to bring down the temperature.

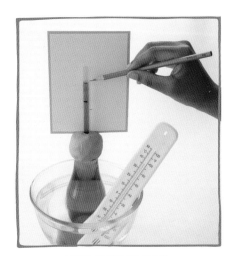

HOT WATER IN BOWL

COLD WATER IN BOWL

# HOW IT WORKS

Water is made of tiny particles called molecules. The molecules are constantly moving about. The higher the temperature, the more vigorously they jiggle, causing the water to expand (take up more space). The only space into which the water can expand is in the straw – that's why the water level rises when your thermometer is put in hot water. As the temperature falls, the molecules move more slowly and take up less space, causing the water level to drop.

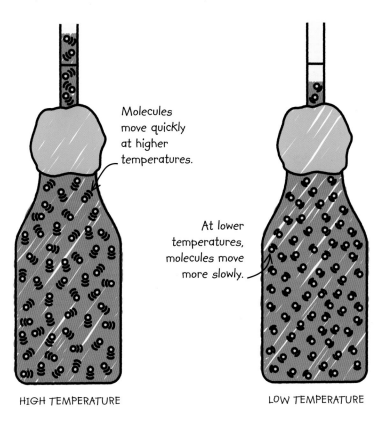

Molecules move quickly at higher temperatures.

At lower temperatures, molecules move more slowly.

HIGH TEMPERATURE                LOW TEMPERATURE

## REAL WORLD SCIENCE
## BODY TEMPERATURE

A liquid thermometer can be used to measure the temperature of a room or check your body's temperature to see if you have an infection. Infections are caused by germs, such as bacteria and viruses,

that reproduce (breed) inside you. When you have an infection, your brain increases your body's temperature to try to slow down the rate at which the germs can reproduce.

# ANEMOMETER

The wind can be anything from a gentle breeze to a very strong gale, but it is really just air in motion. Weather forecasters, or "meteorologists", use a device called an anemometer to measure the wind speed – the speed at which air is moving. You can measure the speed of the wind, too, by making your own anemometer using a ping pong ball and a shoebox.

## MOVING AIR

The wind speed often increases when the weather is about to change from fine to unsettled, wet weather. Why not use your anemometer to keep a record of the wind speed over several days and see how the weather changes?

On the protractor, you can read the angle to which the ping pong ball is pushed.

When the wind blows, it pushes on the ping pong ball.

# HOW TO BUILD AN
# ANEMOMETER

This is quite a complicated project, so take your time and follow the instructions carefully. In this anemometer design, a ping pong ball is suspended on a string inside a cardboard frame made from a shoebox. You'll need to place it in a spot where the wind will push against the ball. The stronger the wind, the further the ping pong ball will move.

Time
1 hour plus drying time

Difficulty
Hard

## WHAT YOU NEED

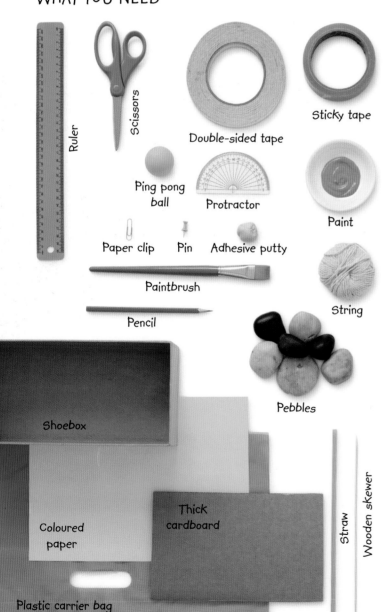

Ruler

Scissors

Double-sided tape

Sticky tape

Ping pong ball

Protractor

Paint

Paper clip

Pin

Adhesive putty

Paintbrush

Pencil

String

Pebbles

Shoebox

Coloured paper

Thick cardboard

Straw

Wooden skewer

Plastic carrier bag

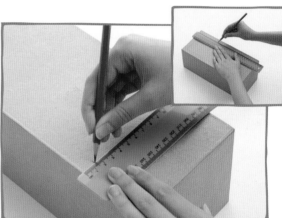

**1** Make a mark 1½ cm (¾ in) in from each edge of the three long faces of the shoebox. Use these marks to draw a rectangle on each face.

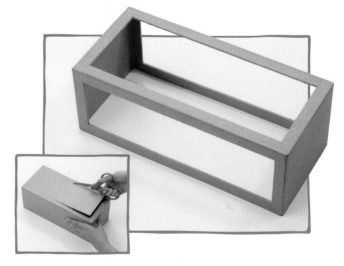

**2** Carefully cut out the rectangle you have drawn on each of the three sides, to create an open frame.

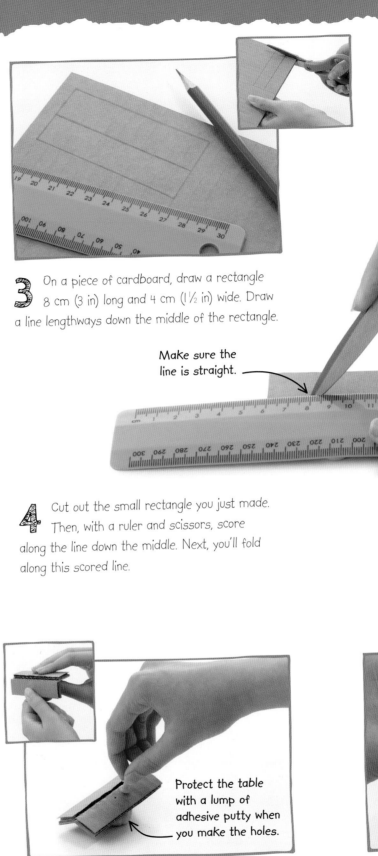

When you score the line, keep the blades of the scissors closed.

**3** On a piece of cardboard, draw a rectangle 8 cm (3 in) long and 4 cm (1½ in) wide. Draw a line lengthways down the middle of the rectangle.

Make sure the line is straight.

**4** Cut out the small rectangle you just made. Then, with a ruler and scissors, score along the line down the middle. Next, you'll fold along this scored line.

Protect the table with a lump of adhesive putty when you make the holes.

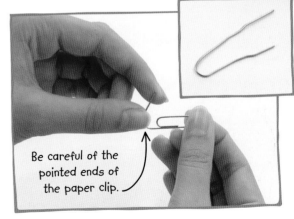

Be careful of the pointed ends of the paper clip.

**5** Using the pin, make two holes on one side of your cardboard rectangle. The holes should be 3.5 cm (1¼ in) from each end of the rectangle and about 1 cm (½ in) apart.

**6** Unfold the paper clip to make a "U" shape. This step is fiddly, so you might want to ask an adult to help you.

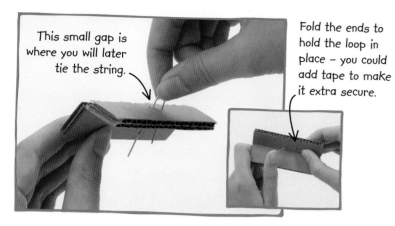

This small gap is where you will later tie the string.

Fold the ends to hold the loop in place – you could add tape to make it extra secure.

**7** Push the paper clip ends through the holes you made and leave a small gap above to create a loop. Fold the two ends outwards.

**8** Draw around the protractor onto coloured paper or use the template at the back of this book. Cut out the semi-circle shape.

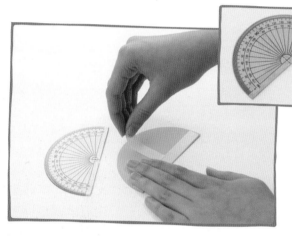

Stick the straight side of the protractor just below the loop.

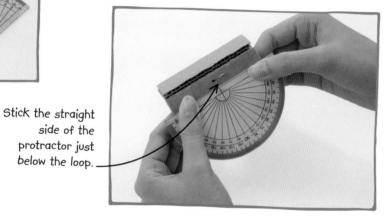

**9** Stick two pieces of double-sided tape onto the semi-circle. Peel off the protective strips and secure the paper to the protractor.

**10** Use another piece of double-sided tape to stick the protractor onto the rectangle so the curved side hangs down.

**11** Now you need one last piece of double-sided tape to make the other side of the cardboard rectangle sticky. Peel off the protective strip.

**12** Attach the cardboard rectangle to the inside of one end of the box, as shown.

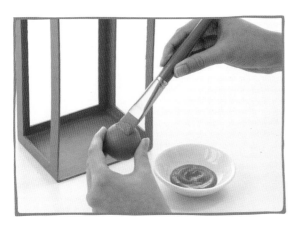

**13** Paint the entire cardboard frame and then the ping pong ball. Don't paint the protractor! Leave them to dry.

Use a piece of adhesive putty to protect the table.

**14** With string taped to its pointed end, poke the skewer through the ping pong ball and out the other side. When the string appears, keep hold of it, then remove the tape, and pull the skewer out. You can now throw the skewer away.

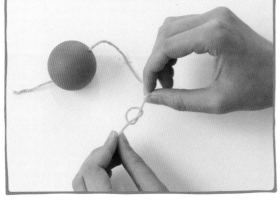

**15** Cut the string so it is long enough for the ping pong ball to hang near the bottom of the frame. Tie a knot at one end of the string to stop the ball falling off.

If this bit is too tricky, ask an adult for help.

**16** Tie the free end of the string around the paper clip loop.

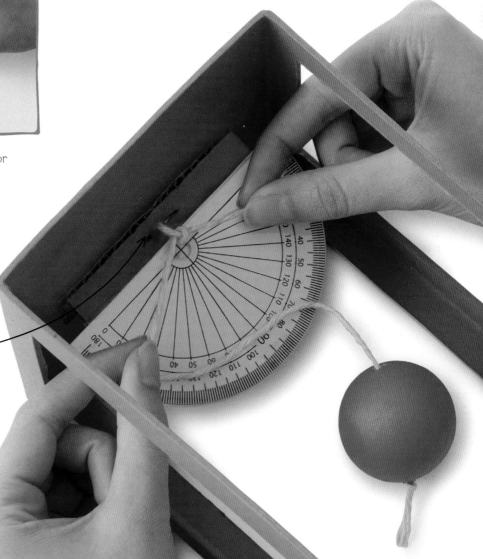

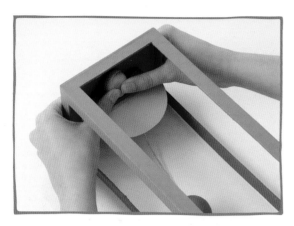

**17** Press a piece of adhesive putty behind where the protractor meets the frame to ensure it hangs down vertically.

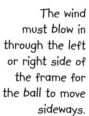

**18** Cut a small flag shape from a plastic bag and stick it to the top of a straw with sticky tape.

**19** Use sticky tape to secure the straw near the top of one edge of the frame. Take your anemometer outside.

Be careful not to leave your anemometer out in wet weather, as the cardboard will bend if it gets wet.

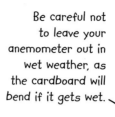

The flag will indicate which way the wind is blowing.

The wind must blow in through the left or right side of the frame for the ball to move sideways.

The pebbles weigh the anemometer down to stop it blowing over.

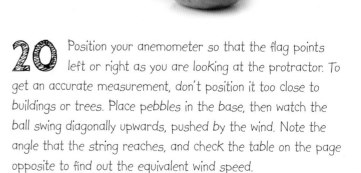

**20** Position your anemometer so that the flag points left or right as you are looking at the protractor. To get an accurate measurement, don't position it too close to buildings or trees. Place pebbles in the base, then watch the ball swing diagonally upwards, pushed by the wind. Note the angle that the string reaches, and check the table on the page opposite to find out the equivalent wind speed.

# HOW IT WORKS

When the wind blows – when air is moving – it pushes the ping pong ball sideways. The ball is supported by the string, so it swings upwards as it is pushed sideways. The faster the wind blows, the stronger the push, and the more the ping pong ball swings upwards. You can estimate the speed of the wind from the angle the string indicates on the protractor, by looking at the table below.

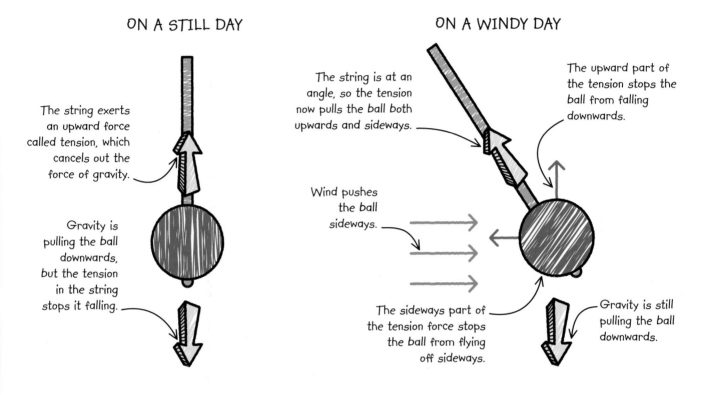

### ON A STILL DAY

The string exerts an upward force called tension, which cancels out the force of gravity.

Gravity is pulling the ball downwards, but the tension in the string stops it falling.

### ON A WINDY DAY

The string is at an angle, so the tension now pulls the ball both upwards and sideways.

The upward part of the tension stops the ball from falling downwards.

Wind pushes the ball sideways.

The sideways part of the tension force stops the ball from flying off sideways.

Gravity is still pulling the ball downwards.

| Angle of string | | 90° | 85° | 80° | 75° | 70° | 65° | 60° | 55° | 50° | 45° | 40° | 35° | 30° | 25° | 20° |
|---|---|---|---|---|---|---|---|---|---|---|---|---|---|---|---|---|
| Wind speed | (km/h) | 0 | 9 | 13 | 16 | 19 | 22 | 24 | 26 | 29 | 32 | 34 | 38 | 42 | 46 | 52 |
| | (mph) | 0 | 5½ | 8 | 10 | 12 | 13½ | 15 | 16 | 18 | 20 | 21 | 23½ | 26 | 28½ | 32 |

# REAL WORLD SCIENCE
## MEASURING WIND SPEED

A weather station is a place where meteorologists (weather forecasters) observe and track weather conditions over time. Meteorologists use a type of anemometer called a cup anemometer, which has three or four cups mounted on a vertical pole. The wind pushes the cups around, which in turn causes a generator attached to the pole to rotate. The faster the wind blows, the more electricity is produced by the generator. A computer analyses the amount of electricity generated to record the wind speed.

# CRACKING ROCKS

This experiment explores "freeze-thaw action", a process that starts when water gets into the tiny cracks of a rock. As the temperature falls at night and rises during the day, this water freezes, then melts... then freezes and melts again. Water is one of the few liquids that expands when it freezes, so, over time, this constant freezing and thawing splits the cracks wider and wider, until eventually even the hardest rock will break into pieces.

The balloon inside this "rock" just has air in it, so the rock didn't break.

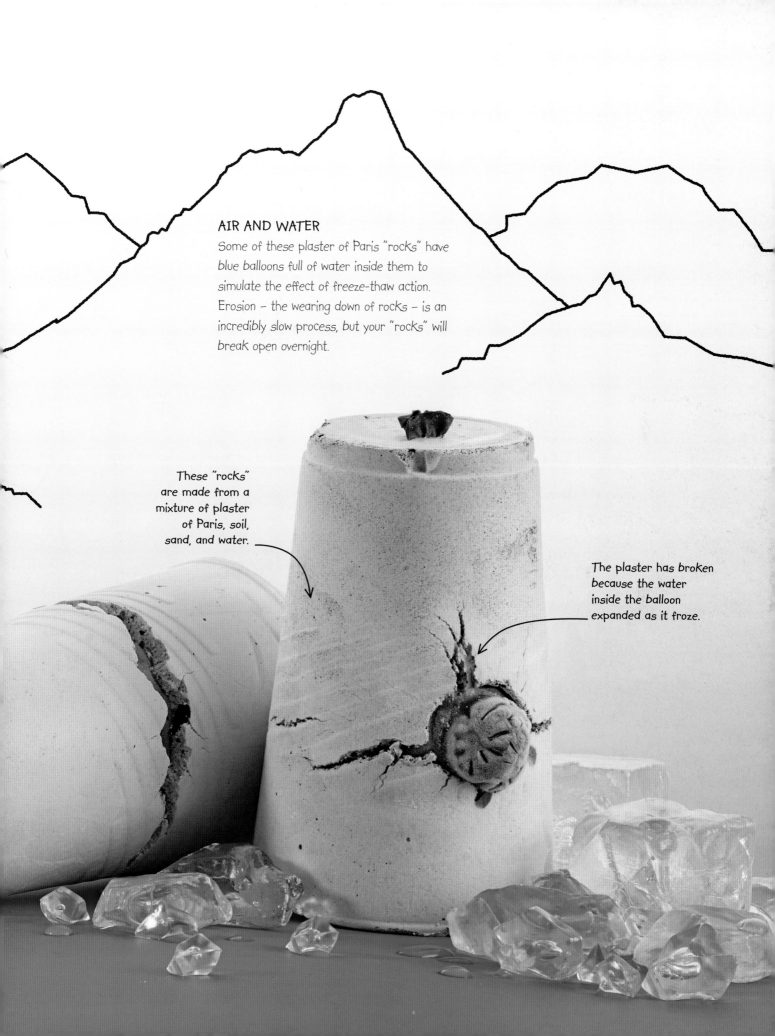

## AIR AND WATER

Some of these plaster of Paris "rocks" have *blue balloons full of water* inside them to simulate the effect of freeze-thaw action. Erosion – the wearing down of rocks – is an incredibly slow process, but your "rocks" will break open overnight.

These "rocks" are made from a mixture of plaster of Paris, soil, sand, and water.

The plaster has broken *because the water inside the balloon expanded as it froze.*

# HOW TO MAKE
# CRACKING ROCKS

This activity needs patience. You'll be leaving the plaster of Paris to set overnight and then keeping it in the freezer the next night. If you have sensitive skin, you should wear protective gloves when handling the plaster of Paris.

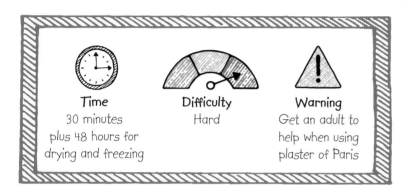

**Time**
30 minutes plus 48 hours for drying and freezing

**Difficulty**
Hard

**Warning**
Get an adult to help when using plaster of Paris

## WHAT YOU NEED

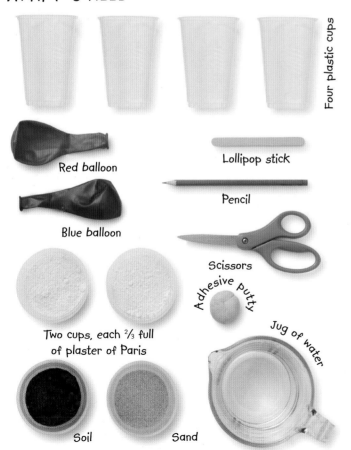

Four plastic cups

Red balloon

Lollipop stick

Blue balloon

Pencil

Scissors

Two cups, each ⅔ full of plaster of Paris

Adhesive putty

Jug of water

Soil

Sand

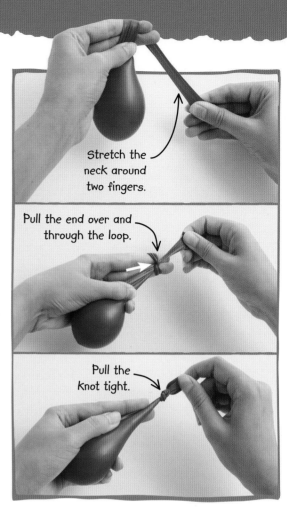

Stretch the neck around two fingers.

Pull the end over and through the loop.

Pull the knot tight.

**1** Blow up the red balloon just a little and tie a knot in its neck. To do this, stretch the neck around two fingers to make a loop, then pass the end over and through that loop, using the groove between your fingers, and pull it tight. If you have trouble, ask an adult for help.

It's best to do this outside or over a sink.

**2** Pour water into the blue balloon, until it's about the same size as the red balloon. Tie a knot in it – try not to spill any water!

**3** Rest a plastic cup on the adhesive putty and make a hole in the bottom using the pencil. Repeat this step with a second cup.

**4** Using the pencil, push the red balloon's knot through the hole in the bottom of one of the cups. Do the same with the blue balloon.

Your two cups now contain a water-filled balloon and a red air-filled balloon.

The putty will hold the balloon in place and seal the hole.

**5** Stand the cups upside down. Make sure the balloons aren't so big that they touch the sides of the cups.

**6** Make two flat discs from adhesive putty and press one firmly over each balloon knot.

**8** Take one of the cups containing plaster of Paris and gradually add water until the plaster is the consistency of thick custard. Mix it with the lollipop stick.

**7** Put each cup you have just prepared inside another cup, to prevent the plaster of Paris leaking in the next step.

The plaster of Paris will bubble and become warm as you add water.

If the plaster becomes too thick, add a little more water and stir.

9 Add some sand and then some soil to your plaster. Mix it well with the lollipop stick.

10 Pour your plaster mixture over the red balloon. Now take the second cup with plaster of Paris in it. Repeat steps 8 and 9, but this time pour the mixture over the blue balloon.

11 You'll now have two cups, each full of plaster, soil, and sand, with the red balloon inside one cup and the blue balloon inside the other. Leave them to set overnight in a place where they won't get knocked over.

12 The next day, the plaster should feel as hard as rock. Remove the outer cups and pull off the adhesive putty covering the balloon knots.

Leave the knot in place.

13 Cut off the excess rubber above the knot of each balloon. Be careful not to cut off the knot itself or the balloons might leak.

14 Cut a slit in each plastic cup with the scissors, and peel away the plastic to leave your "rocks" with the balloon ends sticking out.

Be careful of the sharp edges when cutting off the cup.

**15** Place both rocks in the freezer and leave them there overnight. You could put them on a tray to avoid any mess. The temperature of the water, the air, and the plaster will fall below freezing point. The water in the balloon will freeze.

The rock with the red balloon inside hasn't cracked because the air didn't expand.

**16** The next day, take your two rocks out of the freezer and examine them. You should find the water-filled blue balloon has expanded and broken the plaster.

# HOW IT WORKS

Water is made of extremely tiny particles called molecules. Even in a tiny drop, there are trillions of water molecules. When water is liquid, the molecules move around each other, but when it freezes, they lock together in a regular hexagonal pattern. This pattern takes up more space than the molecules did when the water was liquid, which is why the water expands in the freezer, breaking the plaster. In contrast, air molecules pull closer together as they get colder, so the red balloon doesn't affect the plaster at all.

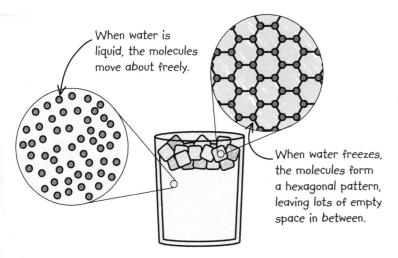

When water is liquid, the molecules move about freely.

When water freezes, the molecules form a hexagonal pattern, leaving lots of empty space in between.

# REAL WORLD SCIENCE
## CRACKED ROCKS

Freeze-thaw action frequently happens in deserts, where the temperature can reach 50°C (122°F) during the day, but regularly falls below freezing at night. Freeze-thaw action doesn't just affect rocks, however. The expansion of water as it freezes can crack water pipes in homes, too. It can even break car engines, so people often put antifreeze into their car engine's cooling system during the winter, which prevents the water from freezing.

# WATER POWER

The experiments in this chapter give you the chance to experiment with perhaps the most important and fascinating substance on Earth: water. As a liquid, water has some amazing properties, and you'll be experimenting with them in lots of different ways – including making your very own giant bubbles. But you'll get to experiment with ice, too, by making your own ice cream!

### FLOATING ABOUT

Small *bubbles* have very tight, perfectly spherical surfaces, and they tend to fall quite quickly to the ground because they contain hardly any air. Bigger *bubbles*, on the other hand, contain loads of air, so they float for longer. The surfaces of big bubbles are less tight than those of smaller *bubbles*, which means they create all sorts of wobbly shapes.

# GIANT BUBBLES

It's wonderful to watch huge, colourful bubbles float gracefully through the air. In this activity, you'll learn how to make a really great bubble mixture and a bubble maker, so you can make enormous, glistening bubbles. These bubbles can make a sticky mess when they burst, so this is definitely an activity you'll need to do outside!

# HOW TO CREATE
# GIANT BUBBLES

You'll have the best chance of making large, long-lasting bubbles if the air is humid, just before or after rainy weather. Air is humid if it has lots of water vapour in it. When there's lots of water in the air, the water in the soap film evaporates much more slowly – that's why the bubbles last longer.

| Time | Difficulty |
|------|------------|
| 90 minutes | Medium |

## WHAT YOU NEED

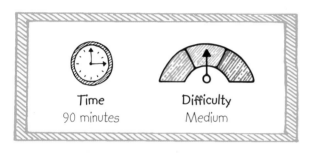

Wooden spoon

Tablespoon of glycerin

Tablespoon of baking powder

½ cup of cornflour

String

Coloured tape

½ cup of washing up liquid

Washer

Five cups of water

Scissors

Two bendy straws

Two garden sticks

Bucket

**1** Add the water to the bucket. The water should be a little bit warm to help the ingredients mix.

**2** Mix the cornflour into the water and stir it in using the wooden spoon. If it sinks to the bottom, just stir it up again.

**3** Pour in the glycerine, baking powder, and washing up liquid. Stir gently, trying not to create too much foam. Leave the mixture to rest for about an hour, but stir it occasionally.

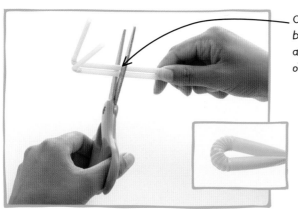

Cut the straws below the bend and fold each one into a loop.

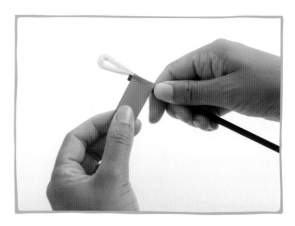

**4** Now you can build the bubble maker. Cut two straws in half, then fold each half in half again at the bendy bit to create a loop.

**5** Press the loop against the top of one garden stick, then tightly wrap a piece of tape around them to hold the loop in place. Repeat for the other garden stick.

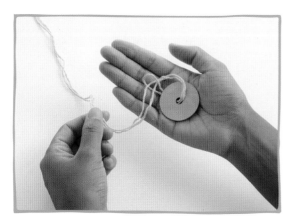

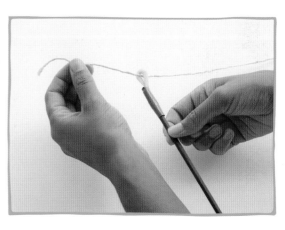

**6** Cut a piece of string 2 m (6½ ft) long. Tie the washer onto the string at the halfway point with a knot or a loop, so that it creates a weight to pull the string down.

**7** Thread one end of the string through each of the loops.

**8** Tie the two ends of the string together so that the string makes a complete loop. Your bubble maker is ready – it's time to make some giant bubbles.

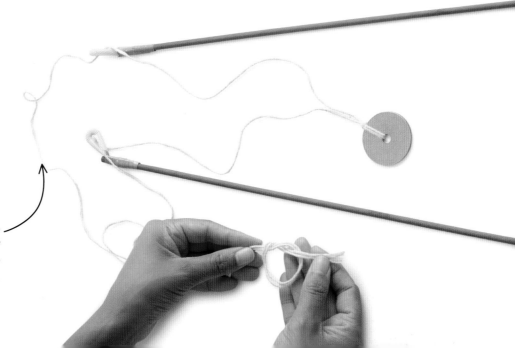

Be careful not to tangle your loop of string while tying the two ends together.

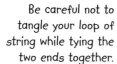

There should be a soapy film inside the loop of string.

**9** Dip the string into the mixture and swirl it around. Lift the string from the bubble mixture by gently pulling the sticks out of the bucket. Keep the sticks fairly close together for now, and make sure the string has been soaked with the mixture.

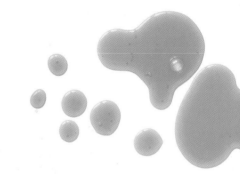

**10** Once you have fully lifted the bubble maker out of the mixture, slowly move the sticks apart. You might need to practise a little bit. As you pull the sticks apart, take a step backwards to trap some air inside the soapy film. To close up a bubble, bring the sticks closer together.

Why not experiment with different string types for the bubble maker, or adding different ingredients to the mixture?

As you pull the sticks apart, the soapy film should stretch.

# TAKE IT FURTHER

Try putting your hand through the soapy film inside the loop of string – the film will burst, but only if your hand is dry. When your dry hand makes a hole in the film, the water pulls back in all directions, and the film breaks. But with a wet hand, the water in the film clings to the water on your hand. When you pull your hand out, the film reseals behind you. The bubble mixture might irritate your skin, so you might want to wear protective gloves for this bit.

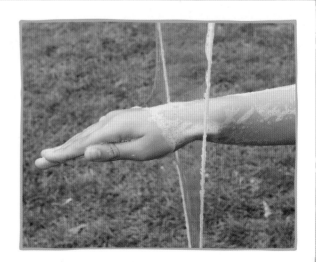

# HOW IT WORKS

A bubble is like a balloon, but instead of stretchy rubber holding the air inside, there is a stretchy film of soapy water. Water by itself won't make a bubble because water molecules cling together too strongly, forming droplets instead of a film. But adding soap changes that. One end of each soap molecule always points away from the water, while the other end of the molecule is attracted to the water. The water ends up trapped inside a very thin sandwich, with soap molecules either side.

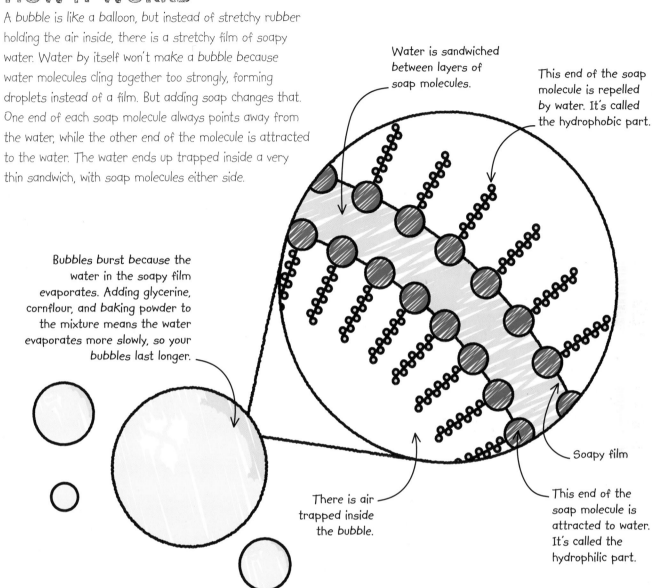

Water is sandwiched between layers of soap molecules.

This end of the soap molecule is repelled by water. It's called the hydrophobic part.

Bubbles burst because the water in the soapy film evaporates. Adding glycerine, cornflour, and baking powder to the mixture means the water evaporates more slowly, so your bubbles last longer.

There is air trapped inside the bubble.

Soapy film

This end of the soap molecule is attracted to water. It's called the hydrophilic part.

## REAL WORLD SCIENCE
### BUBBLES IN NATURE

Bubbles are often found in nature. Some substances produced by plants or animals dissolve in water and act a bit like soap. They form thin films of water and air gets trapped inside. Bubbles happen where there is splashing – like at the bottom of a waterfall – and some animals even produce them on purpose. This violet snail blows bubbles in its mucus to make a floating raft, which it uses to drift across the open sea for hundreds of kilometres.

Air escapes upwards through the middle of the whirlpool, or "vortex".

# SPINNING WHIRLPOOL

When water empties down a plughole or an oar is pulled through water, you'll see spiralling, funnel-shaped whirlpools, or "vortices". These twisting currents also form in lakes, rivers, and the sea, where waves and tides create streams of water moving in opposite directions. With just two plastic bottles, food colouring, strong tape, and some water, you can make your own mesmerizing whirlpool device.

## WHIRLING WATER

These whirlpool devices each use two bottles taped together, one on top of the other. One of the bottles is full of water, and the other is full of air. Turn the device so that the water is collected in the top bottle, and give it a slight shake. The water will start spinning and a whirlpool will form. You can use your device again and again – just turn it the other way round each time!

A force called centripetal force acts on the water, causing it to spin inwards towards the centre.

The water spins fastest at the centre of the vortex.

# HOW TO CREATE A
# SPINNING WHIRLPOOL

These whirlpool devices are a bit like hourglasses, but with water instead of sand. They are easy to make. You will need two large plastic bottles and some coloured water. You'll need to make sure the point where the bottles join is watertight to avoid any leaks.

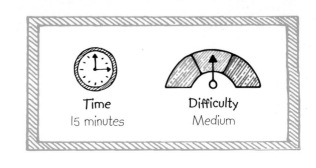

Time
15 minutes

Difficulty
Medium

## WHAT YOU NEED

Strong tape

Adhesive putty

Measuring jug

Food colouring

Two large plastic bottles

Scissors

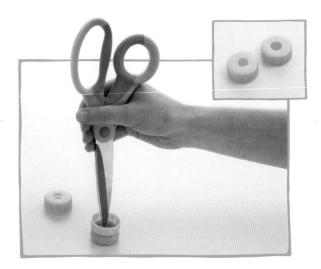

**1** Place a bottle cap upside down on a piece of adhesive putty. Using the scissors, make a neat hole in it about 1 cm (½ in) in diameter with the scissors. Repeat with the other cap.

**2** Fill the measuring jug with water and add some food colouring. You'll need enough water to nearly fill a large bottle, so you'll probably have to fill the jug more than once.

This bottle is full of air.

Fill the bottle nearly to the top.

4 Screw on the caps of both bottles tightly enough to make a watertight seal. An adult can help you screw the cap on tightly.

3 Pour coloured water into one of the bottles, almost to the top. Make sure you do this outside or over a sink. Leave the other bottle empty.

It'll be easier to see the whirlpool with coloured water.

5 Place the bottle that's filled with just air upside down on top of the bottle containing water. Try to line up the holes in the two caps.

Ask an adult to help you with this step.

6 Wrap strong tape around both bottles' lids. Pull it tight, so it holds the bottles firmly together and won't allow water to leak out.

**7** Turn the device upside down. If you don't disturb the water too much, it should stay in the top bottle, even though it's heavier than the air below.

The water is pressing down on the air in the bottom bottle.

If you've taped the bottles securely, they shouldn't leak, but it's a good idea to do this experiment outside, just in case.

The bottom bottle might look empty, but it's not – there is air inside pushing back against the water.

Some water may drip into the bottom bottle as you steady your whirlpool device.

**8** Grasp the bottles and twirl them around. Rotating the bottles causes the water to spin, creating a vortex. The water will slowly begin to pour through the connection.

As the water drains through, what shape does it make?

This whirlpool has already been spinning for a while, so there is lots of water in the bottom bottle.

# HOW IT WORKS

When you first tip the whirlpool device upside down, the water doesn't drain through, even though it's heavier than the air in the bottle below. This is because the bottom bottle is full of air, which presses against the sides of the bottle and also upwards against the water above. This air pressure holds back the water in the top bottle, but once you spin the bottles, you allow the air a way to escape upwards, so the water can drain through to the bottom.

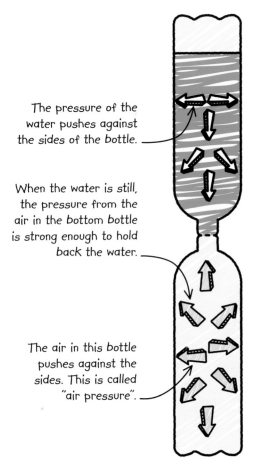

The pressure of the water pushes against the sides of the bottle.

When the water is still, the pressure from the air in the bottom bottle is strong enough to hold back the water.

The air in this bottle pushes against the sides. This is called "air pressure".

Air rushes up to fill the space at the top of the bottle.

A type of force called "centripetal force" causes the water to spin rapidly inwards as it drains, forming a vortex.

As you spin the bottles, the water in the top bottle starts to drain through.

The air travels up through the centre of the vortex.

As the water drains into the bottle below, it displaces (moves) more air upwards.

# REAL WORLD SCIENCE
## TORNADOES

The vortex you've created in your whirlpool bottles looks a lot like another kind of vortex: a tornado. These dangerous and terrifying swirling winds extend down from the base of thunderclouds and can destroy trees, houses, and cars. A tornado forms when a downward current of air from a thundercloud draws in air from all around it, creating a rapidly spinning column with very fast winds.

Stick coloured
pencils through
a bag full of
water without
spilling a drop!

### WHAT IS WATER?

Water is made of extremely tiny particles called
water molecules. These molecules are so small that
even a drop of water is made of trillions and trillions
of them. In liquid water, the molecules move around
each other freely, which is why water flows. But water
molecules also cling to each other, which is why you
see droplets if you spill some water.

# WONDERFUL WATER

We use water every day – to wash, cook, and drink, to water plants, and to swim in. It fills Earth's rivers, lakes, and oceans, and we often see it fall as rain – so we're all familiar with how water feels and behaves. Yet water can still surprise us, as these three activities demonstrate. You'll need to do these experiments outside, or at least over a kitchen sink – you might get wet!

Learn about density with these colourful jars of saltwater.

When these pins are pulled out, what do you think will happen?

# HOW TO MAKE A
# WATERTIGHT WONDER

Here's an amazing science trick that looks like magic: stick pencils right through a plastic bag filled with water... without any of the water leaking out! But do this activity outside because the water will spill when you pull the pencils out. The tricky part is pouring the water into the kitchen bag, so ask someone if they can hold the bag open for you.

**Time**
15 minutes

**Difficulty**
Easy

## WHAT YOU NEED

Clear kitchen bag

Several coloured pencils

Jug of water

**1** Set the bag on a flat surface, then slowly and carefully fill it nearly to the top with water. Ask someone to hold the bag open for you if you need.

**2** Seal the top of the bag tightly and securely, trying not to spill any water.

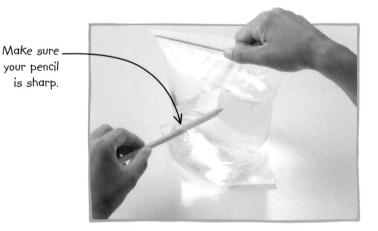

Make sure your pencil is sharp.

**3** Holding the bag at the top with one hand, push a pencil, sharpened end first, through the bag in one smooth movement.

Water molecules are cohesive, which means they are attracted to each other.

When you have finished this activity, recycle the bag if you can.

You should find that no water leaks out at all.

4 Stick all your pencils through the bag one by one. Still no water leaks out! Remember, go outside or hold the bag over a sink when you remove the pencils.

# HOW IT WORKS

Kitchen bags are made of polythene, a strong but flexible material. When the pencil makes a hole through it, the polythene wraps tightly around the pencil, but leaves a tiny gap – a hole through which water could escape. Water molecules cling together, so if a hole is small enough, the clinging force between the water molecules near the hole is strong. If it's stronger than the push from the water molecules inside, the water won't escape. Make the hole much bigger and the molecules can't hold back the pressure from inside, and the water leaks out.

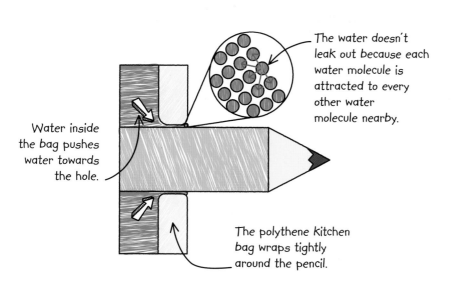

The water doesn't leak out because each water molecule is attracted to every other water molecule nearby.

Water inside the bag pushes water towards the hole.

The polythene kitchen bag wraps tightly around the pencil.

## REAL WORLD SCIENCE
### WATER DROPLETS

The way water molecules pull together explains why water forms round droplets whenever it can. Without a strong pull of gravity, water droplets are perfectly round and hang in the air, like this droplet hanging in the air in the International Space Station.

# HOW TO MAKE
# SALTWATER JARS

In this activity, you will add salt to a cup of water until no more will dissolve. Adding salt increases the density of the water because you've packed more mass (stuff, or "matter") into the same volume (how much space the water takes up). Mixing the salty water with pure water in two different ways will give surprising results.

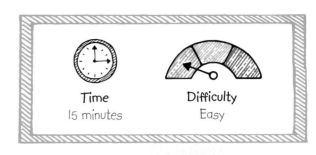

**Time**
15 minutes

**Difficulty**
Easy

## WHAT YOU NEED

Two cups of water

Red food colouring

Blue food colouring

½ cup of salt

Spoon

Two glass jars

**1** Pour blue food colouring into one of the plastic cups of water. Stir it with the spoon until the water is completely blue.

**2** Pour red food colouring into the other cup of water and use the spoon to stir it.

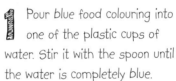
Add salt until no more dissolves.

**3** Add salt to the red water and stir it to help it dissolve. You've added enough salt when no more will dissolve.

**4** Pour half the blue non-salty water into one of the glass jars, and half the red salty water into the other.

**5** Now it's time to top up the jar containing *blue* water. So you don't disturb it, slowly add the rest of the *red* water into the jar by pouring it over the back of the spoon.

**6** Carefully pour the rest of the *blue* water onto the back of the spoon and into the jar containing the red water.

**7** Let the two jars stand for a while. You should see that in one jar the two colours mix together, but in the other jar the colours remain separate.

# HOW IT WORKS

Adding salt to the red water hardly changes its volume, but it does add lots of mass, making it denser than the blue non-salty water. When the denser red water is poured on top of the blue water, it sinks through it and the two colours mix. When you pour the other way round – the red water before blue – the blue water floats on top because it has been placed on a liquid with a higher density.

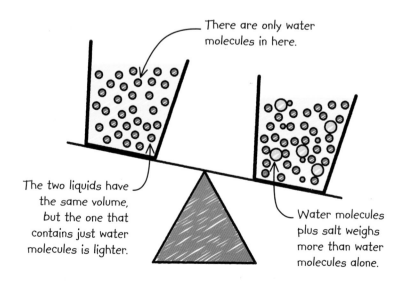

There are only water molecules in here.

The two liquids have the same volume, but the one that contains just water molecules is lighter.

Water molecules plus salt weighs more than water molecules alone.

## REAL WORLD SCIENCE
### UNDERWATER LAKES

In this picture, the diver is swimming above a lake of very salty water – but that lake is underwater! Just as happened in the activity, the salty water stays at the bottom because it is more dense than the fresh water above it. Salty water is called brine, and underwater lakes of salty water are called brine pools.

# HOW TO MAKE A
# PIN BOTTLE

Learn how to make water defy gravity! You can make holes in a full bottle of water without the water leaking out, as long as the cap stays firmly closed. This simple but surprising activity lets you explore the forces of water pressure and air pressure. Make sure you recycle the bottle after you finish the experiment.

**Time**
15 minutes

**Difficulty**
Easy

## WHAT YOU NEED

Bottle full of water

Pins

**1** Take your bottle full of water and poke a pin carefully through the bottle near the bottom, leaving the pin in place.

Water can't escape because the pins block the holes they made.

**2** Add more pins, pushing them straight in, not at an angle. You can put the pins wherever you like. We put them in a line near the bottom of the bottle.

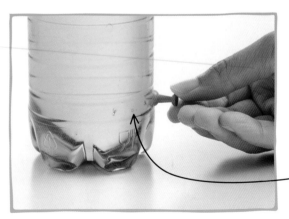

Does any water leak out?

**3** Now for the tricky bit. Carefully remove the pins one by one. Pull them straight out, not at an angle, so that the holes they leave behind are small and round.

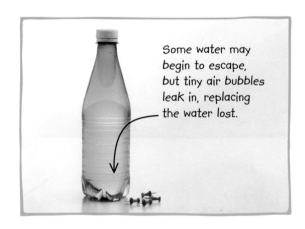

Some water may begin to escape, but tiny air bubbles leak in, replacing the water lost.

**4** Once all the pins are out, watch the bottle for a few moments. You should find that almost no water escapes, despite the fact that there are holes in the bottle.

## HOW IT WORKS

There are two forces acting on the water at the bottom of the bottle, just inside the holes. Firstly, there is atmospheric pressure – the push of the air outside the bottle. Secondly, there is the force of the water at the top of the bottle, which eventually pushes the water at the bottom through the pin holes. Atmospheric pressure is enough to stop the water escaping through the holes... until you unscrew the cap. When the cap is removed, air rushes into the bottle. This air pushes down on the top of the water, which causes it to start leaking out.

### CAP ON THE BOTTLE

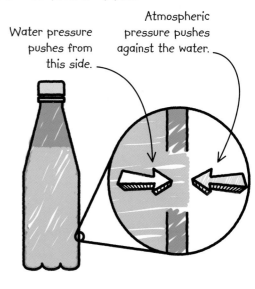

Water pressure pushes from this side.

Atmospheric pressure pushes against the water.

### CAP OFF THE BOTTLE

When you unscrew the cap, air rushes into the bottle, pushing down on the water.

Water streams out of the pin holes – that's why it's best to do this outside!

Atmospheric pressure stops the water streaming out.

**5** Try to do this step over a sink or outside, if you can, as it's messy. Unscrew the bottle's cap. Water will start pouring out through the holes!

What happens when you make the holes vertically above each other instead of horizontally alongside each other?

Water streams out, pushed down by the water above.

# ICE CREAM

Everyone knows that a tasty bowl of ice cream is a delicious treat on a hot summer's day. But did you know that making your own ice cream is even more fun than eating it? All you need is some science, a few simple ingredients – milk, cream, and sugar – and lots of energy to shake and mix the ingredients together. You can even add chocolate chips or strawberries to recreate your favourite flavours, and sprinkles for decoration.

This experiment makes vanilla ice cream, but you can try other flavours, too.

### TASTY TREAT

Ice cream is a mixture of milk and cream that has been cooled to below freezing. As the temperature drops, the water in the milk and cream freezes into tiny ice crystals, giving the ice cream its distinctive texture.

Add sprinkles or sweets to your ice cream for extra crunch.

Small pieces of strawberry in your mixture will give your ice cream a splash of colour.

# HOW TO MAKE
# ICE CREAM

This mouth-watering activity is straightforward but it can get a little messy, so it's best to do it outside. First of all, before handling the ingredients, you'll need to wash your hands. And remember to check that all of the bags are securely sealed before shaking and throwing, so that none of your ice cream mixture or salty ice escapes.

| Time | Difficulty |
|------|-----------|
| 40 minutes | Medium |

## WHAT YOU NEED

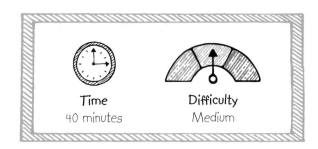

Two tea towels

A dash of vanilla essence

50 g (2 fl oz) sugar

180 ml (6 fl oz) double cream

180 ml (6 fl oz) milk

150 g (5 oz) rock salt

One large kitchen bag

Two small kitchen bags

Plastic carrier bag

A big bowl of ice

**1** Hold open one of the small kitchen bags and pour the double cream into it. Cream is made of water, with droplets, or globules, of fat mixed in.

**2** Pour the milk into the same bag. Like cream, milk is mostly water, but it has fewer globules of fat.

**3** To make your ice cream taste sweet, add the sugar. The sugar helps stop the ice crystals that form in the mixture from getting too big.

Seal part of the bag, then squeeze the air out the gap.

Make sure both bags are sealed securely. You can add tape if you need to.

**4** The final ingredient is a dash of vanilla essence. You don't need to stir the bag's contents, but be sure to gently squeeze out the air before sealing it securely.

**5** Place the bag containing the ingredients in the second small bag. Protecting the ice cream mixture inside an extra bag ensures that it won't mix with any of the ice and salt you'll use next.

Carefully pour the ice into the large empty bag.

**6** Fill the large kitchen bag with ice, then put your bag of ice cream ingredients inside. The ice will start to draw heat from the milk and cream immediately, but on its own, it won't take enough heat away to freeze the ice cream.

**7** When your ice cream mixture is nestled in among the ice, pour in the salt and seal the bag. Putting salt into the bag causes the ice to draw much more heat away from the milk and cream. In fact, the temperature of the ice can drop to a chilly -21°C (-6°F), so be careful not to touch it.

Tip the salt into the large kitchen bag, over the ice.

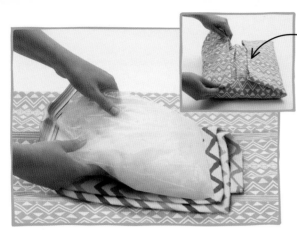

Inside, the ice and salt mixture is already drawing heat from the milk and cream.

A thick plastic carrier bag is best.

**8** Wrap the bag in a double layer of tea towels like a parcel. This will protect your hands from getting too cold and make your ice cream mixture easier to throw and catch, too.

**9** Place the parcel into a plastic carrier bag, keeping the tea towels tightly wrapped around the sealed bag of ice.

Ice cream is a mixture of solids, liquids, and gases.

**10** Tie a knot in the open end of the carrier bag, and then shake, massage, whirl, and throw the bag around for about 15 minutes. Keep the mixture moving while it cools, otherwise the ice crystals in the milk and cream will grow too large, and the ice cream won't be smooth and creamy.

**11** Wash your hands, then untie the carrier bag and unwrap the tea towels. Carefully unseal the large kitchen bag to avoid spilling any melted ice. Finally, take out the smaller bags and open them to reveal your very own homemade ice cream!

If the ice cream is too soft, seal everything back up and shake it for a few more minutes.

# TAKE IT FURTHER

The steps in this experiment will make enough vanilla ice cream to share with three friends, but if you want to make more, just double the amounts of the ingredients, and use bigger kitchen bags. For a bit of variety, and to make your vanilla ice cream taste even better, try introducing different flavours by putting little pieces of fresh fruit or chocolate chips into the mixture before freezing it. Once it's ready to eat, serve up your scoops of ice cream with a wafer, or in a cone if you fancy one.

# HOW IT WORKS

There are three states of matter: solid, liquid, and gas. Even though its temperature is below freezing, ice cream is actually not a solid. It's a type of substance called a colloid: a mixture in which small bits of one substance are mixed evenly into another. Ice cream is made of ice crystals (solid), fats (liquid), and tiny bubbles of air (gas). Shaking it about while it cools down means the ice crystals don't grow too big, ensuring your ice cream is smooth and creamy.

### ICE CREAM MADE BY SHAKING

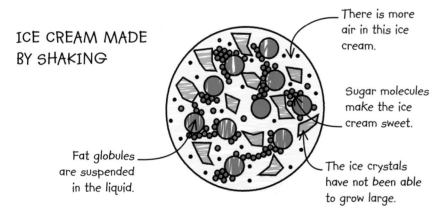

There is more air in this ice cream.

Sugar molecules make the ice cream sweet.

Fat globules are suspended in the liquid.

The ice crystals have not been able to grow large.

### ICE CREAM MADE WITHOUT SHAKING

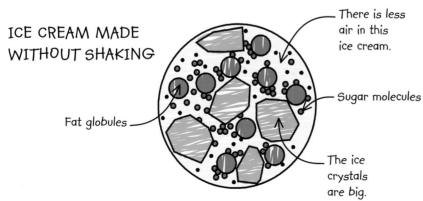

There is less air in this ice cream.

Sugar molecules

Fat globules

The ice crystals are big.

## REAL WORLD SCIENCE
## TYPES OF COLLOID

Many of the substances we use every day are different types of colloid. Whipped cream is a type of colloid called a foam: a mixture of tiny gas bubbles in liquid. Mayonnaise is a mixture of tiny droplets of oil in water, a colloid known as an emulsion. Mist and fog are made of tiny water droplets suspended in the air. This type of colloid is called an aerosol.

# MARBLED PEBBLES

Add splodges of shiny nail varnish to a bowl of water and then dip in pebbles to create these swirly, marble-effect patterns. These pebbles will make a unique gift or an eye-catching display for the garden. It's possible because nail varnish is immiscible with water – this means they won't mix. Instead, the varnish floats in a colourful film on the water's surface, ready for you to dip in your pebble.

The bright patterns on these pebbles are made by dipping them in nail varnish and water.

### COLOURFUL PIGMENTS

Nail varnish is a suspension: a liquid containing tiny droplets or solid particles that are hanging, or "suspended", so that they don't easily settle. The suspended particles are tiny grains of pigment, the compounds that give the varnish its colour.

# HOW TO CREATE
# MARBLED PEBBLES

Most nail varnishes are very smelly, and breathing too much in can be harmful. Because of this, try to do this activity outside on a dry day or in a well-ventilated room. Also, put paper down, in case you knock over a bottle. If you do spill some nail varnish, ask an adult to help clear it up.

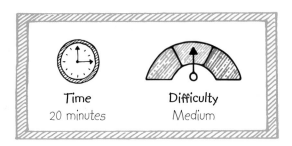

**Time**
20 minutes

**Difficulty**
Medium

## WHAT YOU NEED

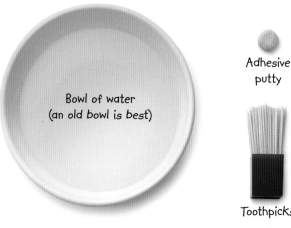

Bowl of water
(an old bowl is best)

Adhesive putty

Toothpicks

Different-coloured nail varnishes

Pebbles

**1** Before you begin, press the adhesive putty onto one side of a pebble. This will act as a handle, so you won't get nail varnish on your fingers.

You may want to wear protective gloves for this bit.

**2** Pour small amounts of different colours of nail varnish onto the surface of the water. Keep the varnish in the middle of the bowl. Gel varnishes won't work in this experiment.

Dispose of the toothpick when you have finished using it.

**3** Use the end of a toothpick to swirl the colours gently around to create a pattern. Be quick as the varnish will soon dry.

**4** Pick up the pebble by its adhesive putty handle, and dip the pebble gently through the layer of nail varnish into the water.

**5** After just a second or two, slowly lift the pebble from the water, and hold it above the surface for a few seconds for water to drip off it.

The varnish film sticks onto the pebble, leaving the water clear.

**6** Turn over the pebble and push the other end of the putty onto a surface. Leave this pebble to dry. Then try again with another pebble!

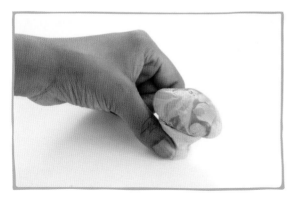

# HOW IT WORKS

Nail varnish is less dense than water, which is why it floats on, but won't dissolve in, water – the two substances are immiscible (un-mixable). Nail varnish contains three main ingredients: a pigment (this gives the varnish its colour), film-forming molecules (which form a hard protective film), and a solvent (a liquid in which all the other ingredients dissolve). The solvent evaporates quickly into the air, giving nail varnish its smell and allowing it to dry quickly.

## CROSS-SECTION OF PEBBLE

Colour pigment (pink) and film-forming molecules (green) are suspended in the solvent (yellow).

The solvent evaporates.

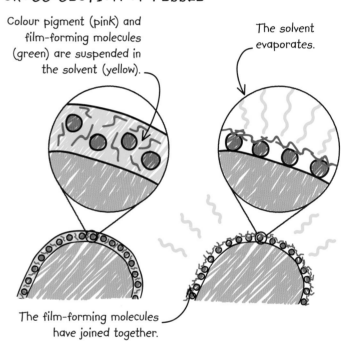

The film-forming molecules have joined together.

## REAL WORLD SCIENCE
## OIL SPILLS

Crude oil, from which petrol and most plastics are made, is immiscible with water. When large ships carrying crude oil spill some, the oil floats on the ocean's surface. The oil sticks to the feathers of seabirds, and it can poison turtles and whales that come to the surface and swallow it.

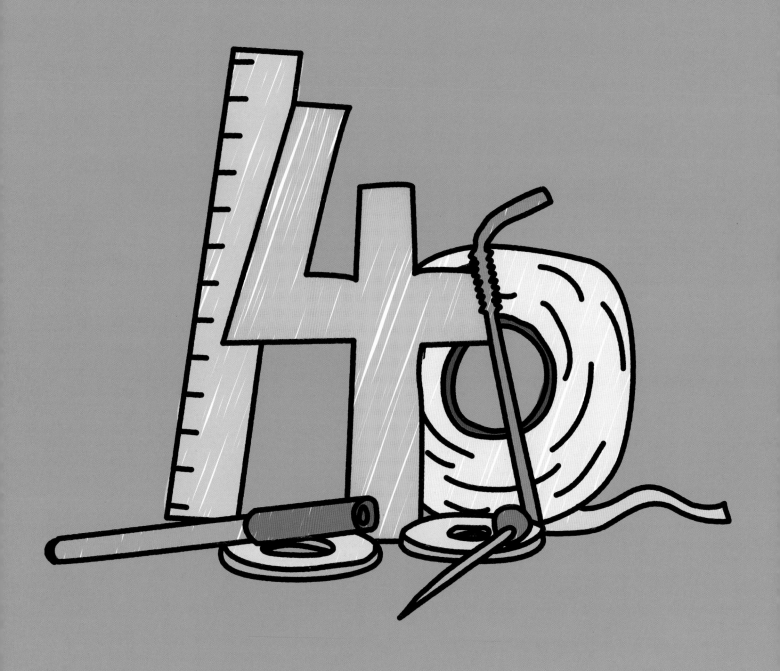

# EARTH AND SKY

The great outdoors! In this chapter, you'll be reaching for the sky – and finding out about the forces the air exerts – by making helicopters, a kite, and even a rocket! You'll also learn about planet Earth, with a sundial that tells the time using the Sun's position in the sky and a magnetic compass that will help you find your way. You'll also make beautiful mineral crystals called geodes that normally form over thousands or millions of years!

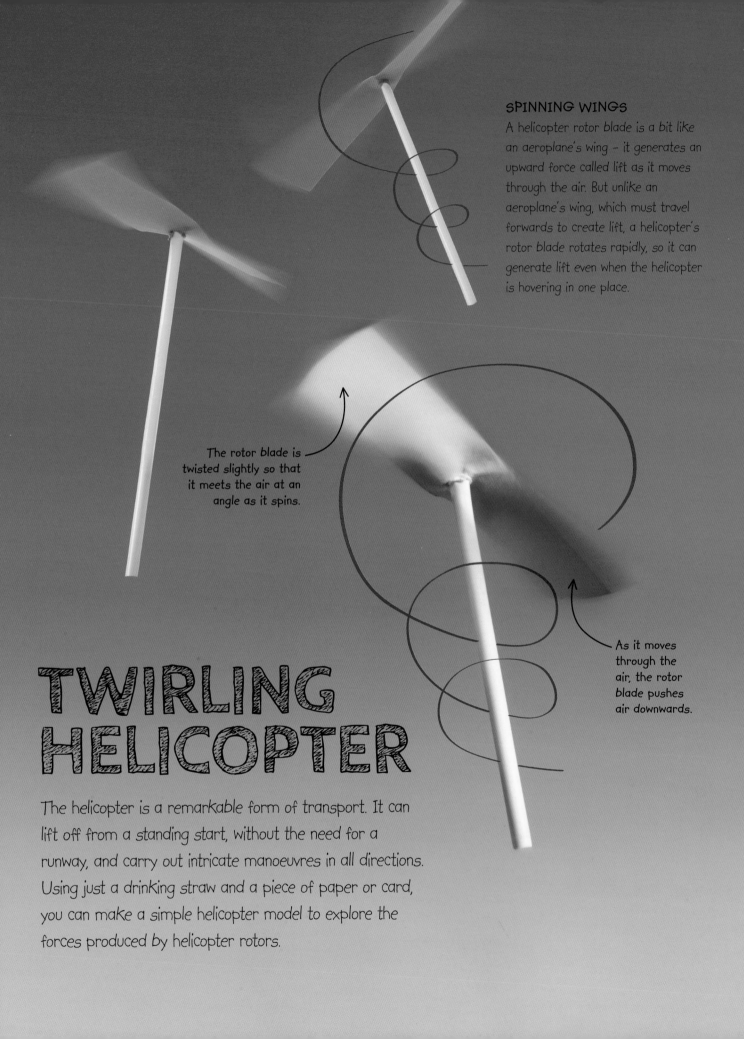

## SPINNING WINGS

A helicopter rotor blade is a bit like an aeroplane's wing – it generates an upward force called lift as it moves through the air. But unlike an aeroplane's wing, which must travel forwards to create lift, a helicopter's rotor blade rotates rapidly, so it can generate lift even when the helicopter is hovering in one place.

The rotor blade is twisted slightly so that it meets the air at an angle as it spins.

As it moves through the air, the rotor blade pushes air downwards.

# TWIRLING HELICOPTER

The helicopter is a remarkable form of transport. It can lift off from a standing start, without the need for a runway, and carry out intricate manoeuvres in all directions. Using just a drinking straw and a piece of paper or card, you can make a simple helicopter model to explore the forces produced by helicopter rotors.

# HOW TO MAKE A
# TWIRLING HELICOPTER

Follow the instructions to make your own helicopter. It might need a bit of flight testing and adjustment. A snip off the ends of the rotor blade, or a slightly longer straw, could make all the difference. You can also test how different weights of paper and card affect your helicopter's flight.

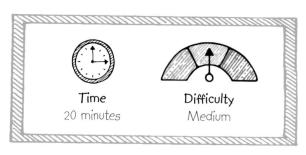

**Time**
20 minutes

**Difficulty**
Medium

## WHAT YOU NEED

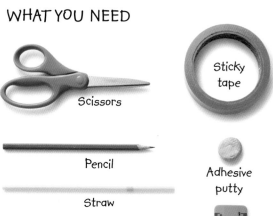

Scissors

Sticky tape

Pencil

Adhesive putty

Straw

Coloured paper or card

Ruler

**1** If you have a bendy straw, cut it off just below the bend. You'll need a straight piece of straw to make your helicopter stable as it flies.

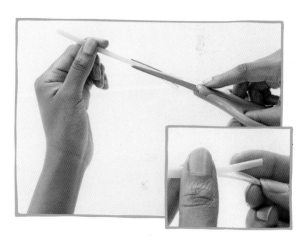

**2** Using the scissors, cut into the end of the straight piece of straw to a depth of about 1 cm (½ in). This will create two tabs that will hold the rotor blade in place.

You'll also find a template at the back of this book that you could trace, if you prefer.

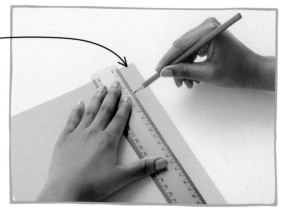

**3** To make the rotor blade, lay the paper or card on a table and draw a rectangle in one corner, 2 cm (1 in) wide by 14 cm (5½ in) long.

**4** Cut out the rectangle you drew on the paper or card, trying not to bend it at this stage.

Measure 1 cm (½ in) in if you want to make sure you are exactly in the centre.

**5** Measure halfway along the long side of the rectangle you just cut out – 7 cm (2¾ in) from one end – and make a mark in the centre.

**6** Place your rotor blade on top of the adhesive putty. Use the sharp end of a pencil to make a hole at the centre point you have marked.

Try not to bend the rotor blade at this stage.

**7** Push the cut end of the straw through the hole. If the hole is not quite big enough, carefully make it a bit bigger with the pencil.

**8** Bend the two halves of the end of the straw in opposite directions and push them flat onto the rotor blade. Secure them with tape. Keep the rotor blade flat.

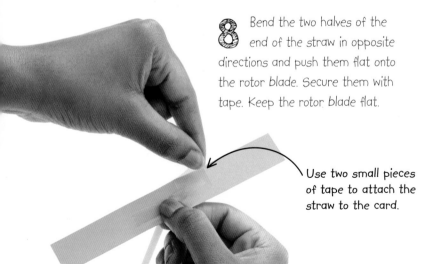

Use two small pieces of tape to attach the straw to the card.

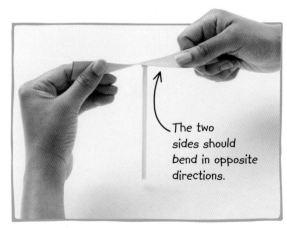

The two sides should bend in opposite directions.

**9** Now, finally, you can bend the rotor blade – otherwise your helicopter won't take off. Gently twist clockwise with each hand.

**10** Your helicopter is ready! To make it fly, you need to hold the straw between your two palms, push your right palm forwards, and release.

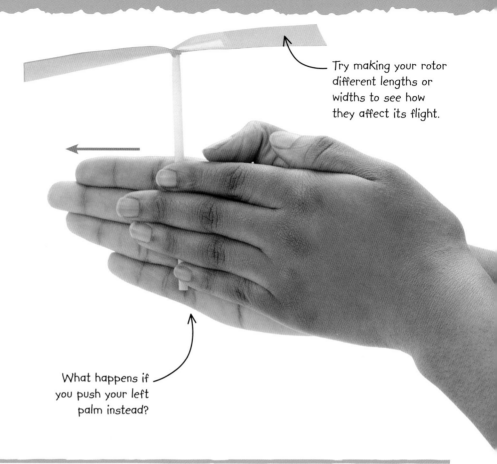

Try making your rotor different lengths or widths to see how they affect its flight.

A helicopter rotor pushes air downwards to create upward lift.

What happens if you push your left palm instead?

# HOW IT WORKS

As the helicopter's rotor blade spins, its angled edges push the surrounding air downwards, creating an area of high pressure air below it (and lower pressure above it). The higher pressure air pushes the rotor blade upwards. This force is called "lift". Try making different helicopters to find the best combination of the length and width of the rotor, how much it is bent, and the length of the straw.

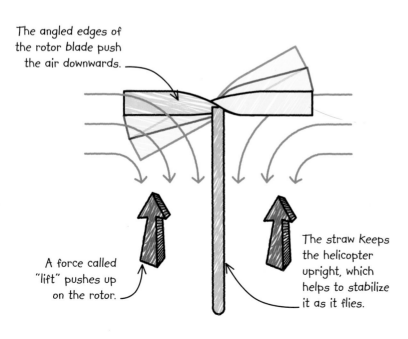

The angled edges of the rotor blade push the air downwards.

A force called "lift" pushes up on the rotor.

The straw keeps the helicopter upright, which helps to stabilize it as it flies.

## REAL WORLD SCIENCE
## UNPILOTED AERIAL VEHICLES

Unpiloted aerial vehicles (UAVs, or drones) have rotor blades similar to your helicopter. Electric motors propel the rotor blades, keeping them spinning – and generating lift. The faster they turn, the more lift they generate. To make the UAV change direction, the rotors on one side turn faster than the rotors on the other side.

The part of the kite that catches the wind is called the sail.

All kites need bridles: a triangular-shaped string arrangement that keeps the kite's sail at a right angle to the flying line.

This is the flying line. Hold tight – it keeps the kite from flying away.

# DIAMOND KITE

When a breeze picks up, there's no better way to experience the power of wind than to fly a kite. The wind can take a kite soaring up high, while you're in control of it down on the ground. In this activity, you can make your own colourful kite that really flies, using things you have at home. If you are inspired by flying your kite, there are lots of other designs you can try. What about using different materials to make the sail? How about making a kite that's much bigger, or one that has a much longer string?

## LET'S GO FLY A KITE

Kite flying can take practice and patience, but you'll find it's worth the effort. A beach is a good place to fly a kite, if it isn't too crowded, because it often has steady breezes. Don't fly a kite in a storm or if it's really windy, and never fly a kite near power lines or airports.

The tail will flutter in the wind.

# HOW TO MAKE A
# DIAMOND KITE

To make the sail of your kite, which catches the wind, you need to use something light, flat, and flexible. This kite is made from two plastic carrier bags. You'll need two sticks that must be strong but flexible, and lots of string to tether the kite as it climbs into the sky!

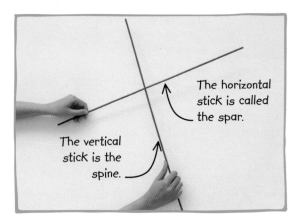

The vertical stick is the spine.

The horizontal stick is called the spar.

**1** Place the two sticks at right angles to each other, with the horizontal one (the spar) a little more than halfway up the vertical stick (the spine).

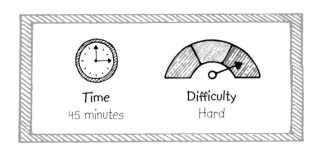

**Time**
45 minutes

**Difficulty**
Hard

## WHAT YOU NEED

Pencil

Felt-tip pen

Adhesive putty

String

Scissors

Double-sided tape

Sticky tape

Two garden sticks

Ruler

Two plastic carrier bags

**2** Cut about 40 cm (16 in) of string, which you'll use to tie the spar and the spine together.

**3** Wrap the string a few times around the crossing point, then tie the sticks together. They should still be at right angles to each other, with the spar a little more than halfway up the spine.

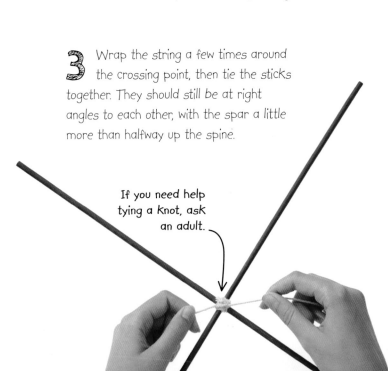

If you need help tying a knot, ask an adult.

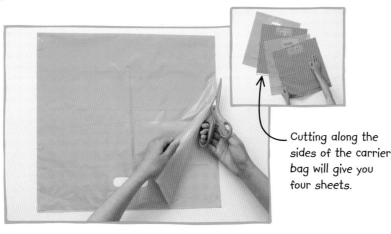

Cutting along the sides of the carrier bag will give you four sheets.

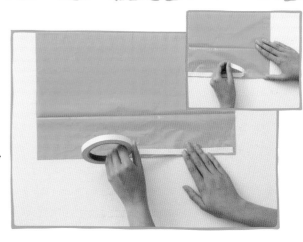

**4** Cut open both sides of each carrier bag, and then across the bottom, so that you end up with four pieces the same size and shape.

**5** Stick double-sided tape along the bottom of one of the bags. Make it as flat as you can. Peel back the protective layer.

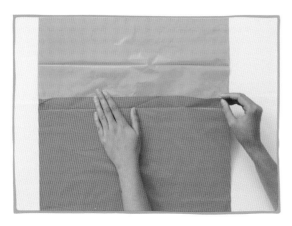

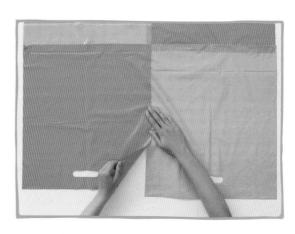

**6** Attach a differently coloured piece of plastic by carefully placing it onto the double-sided tape on the first piece and pressing down.

**7** Make a patchwork pattern as shown with all four pieces stuck together with double-sided tape. Make each join as smooth as possible.

If the spar and the spine are at right angles, they should line up with the joins.

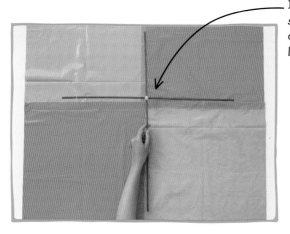

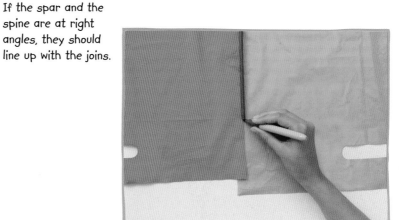

**8** Lay the crossed sticks onto the patchwork pattern, so that the point at which the sticks cross is on top of the centre of the plastic pieces.

**9** With the sticks still in place, mark the position of each end of each stick with the felt-tip pen. Then put the sticks to one side.

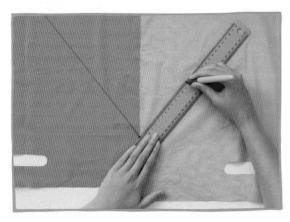

**10** Using a ruler and the felt-tip pen, draw straight lines between the four marks you just made to create the outline of your sail.

Keep these pieces of plastic – you'll need them to make the tail for your kite.

**11** Cut neatly along the straight lines to reveal your diamond-shaped sail.

**12** Carefully lay the crossed sticks on the sail so that the ends of the sticks line up with the points of the diamond shape.

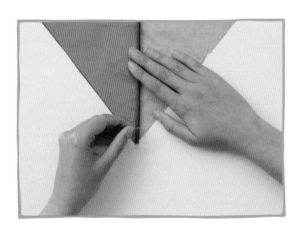

**13** Secure the ends of the sticks to the sail with tape. Make sure they are stuck firmly, as otherwise your kite may fall apart in the wind!

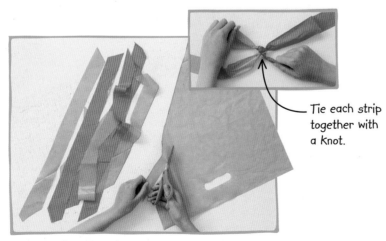

Tie each strip together with a knot.

**14** To make the tail, cut strips from the leftover pieces of plastic and tie the strips together, alternating the colours.

**15** Knot one end of the tail tightly to the spine, and slide it down to the bottom.

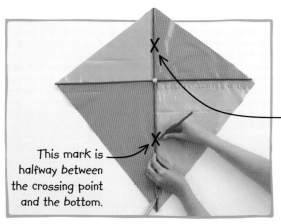

This mark is halfway between the crossing point and the bottom.

Here's the halfway mark between the top of the kite and the crossing point.

**16** Mark one point halfway between the top, or nose, and the crossing point of the kite. Then add a second point halfway between the crossing point and the bottom, or tail. Place adhesive putty underneath and make a small hole in the sail at each mark using the pencil.

**17** Cut a piece of string as long as the kite's spine, and pass the ends through the holes in the plastic sheet. Tie the string to the spine at the two points you marked.

This is the point where you will attach the flying line.

This part, which makes the kite fly at an angle, is called the bridle.

**18** Turn the kite over and pull the string over to one side, moving your fingers along the string until they are over the spar. Keep hold of the string.

A kite is flown at an angle to the wind, so that air is forced underneath it.

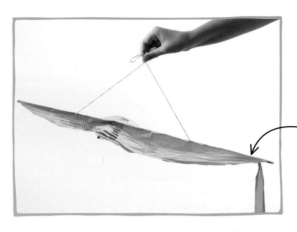

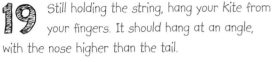

— The tail end
of the kite
should be lower
than the nose.

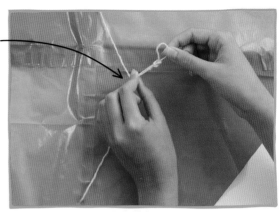

Ask an adult for
help if you find
this too fiddly.

**19** Still holding the string, hang your kite from your fingers. It should hang at an angle, with the nose higher than the tail.

**20** Tie a small loop in the string at the point you were holding with your fingers. This is where you will attach the flying line.

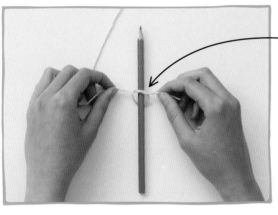

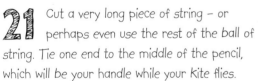

Make sure
the string
is securely
attached to
the pencil.

**21** Cut a very long piece of string – or perhaps even use the rest of the ball of string. Tie one end to the middle of the pencil, which will be your handle while your kite flies.

**22** Wind the entire length of string around the pencil. As the kite climbs higher in the air, you'll be able to let out more string.

**23** Tie the other end of the long piece of string to the loop you made in the bridle. Now your kite is ready to fly! On a breezy day, and never in a storm, take your kite out to an open space – on high ground is ideal.

# HOW IT WORKS

The wind that lifts your kite is simply moving air. Because your kite is at an angle, the moving air is forced downwards under the sail. As the kite pushes the air downwards, the air pushes the kite upwards – this force is called "lift". While the wind is pushing the kite both upwards and forwards, the flying line that you hold pulls the kite downwards and backwards. The stronger the wind, the more you have to tug on the kite to stop it flying away, but if the wind stops or you let go, gravity will bring the kite back down to earth with a crash.

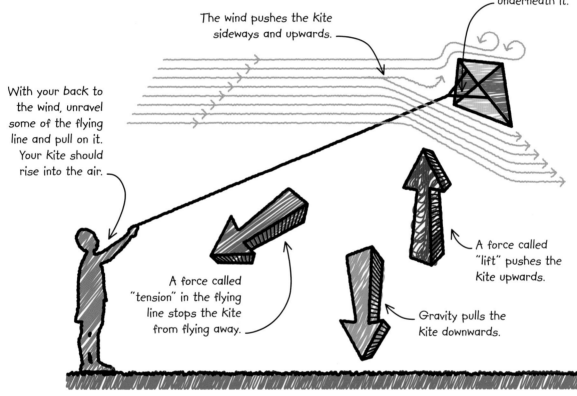

The bridle ensures that the kite flies at an angle to the wind. The angle of the kite forces the wind underneath it.

The wind pushes the kite sideways and upwards.

With your back to the wind, unravel some of the flying line and pull on it. Your kite should rise into the air.

A force called "tension" in the flying line stops the kite from flying away.

A force called "lift" pushes the kite upwards.

Gravity pulls the kite downwards.

## REAL WORLD SCIENCE
## KITESURFING

A kitesurfer uses a large sports kite attached to their waist to speed through the sea on a surfboard. A sports kite is a bit more complicated than your kite. It has two strings instead of just one, which allows the person flying it more control. Pulling on one string or the other makes the kite twist and turn, changing its direction as the air flows over each side of the kite differently. The sports kite can lift the kitesurfer high into the air to perform difficult tricks, such as jumps, flips, and spins.

# WATER ROCKET

Five... four... three... two... one... blast off! You can make a powerful rocket that shoots up into the air at high speed, without using a drop of rocket fuel! This rocket uses air, water, and muscle power to launch a plastic bottle high into the air. Your rocket won't quite reach the stars, but you'll be impressed at how fast and high it can go. So, gather what you need and prepare for lift-off.

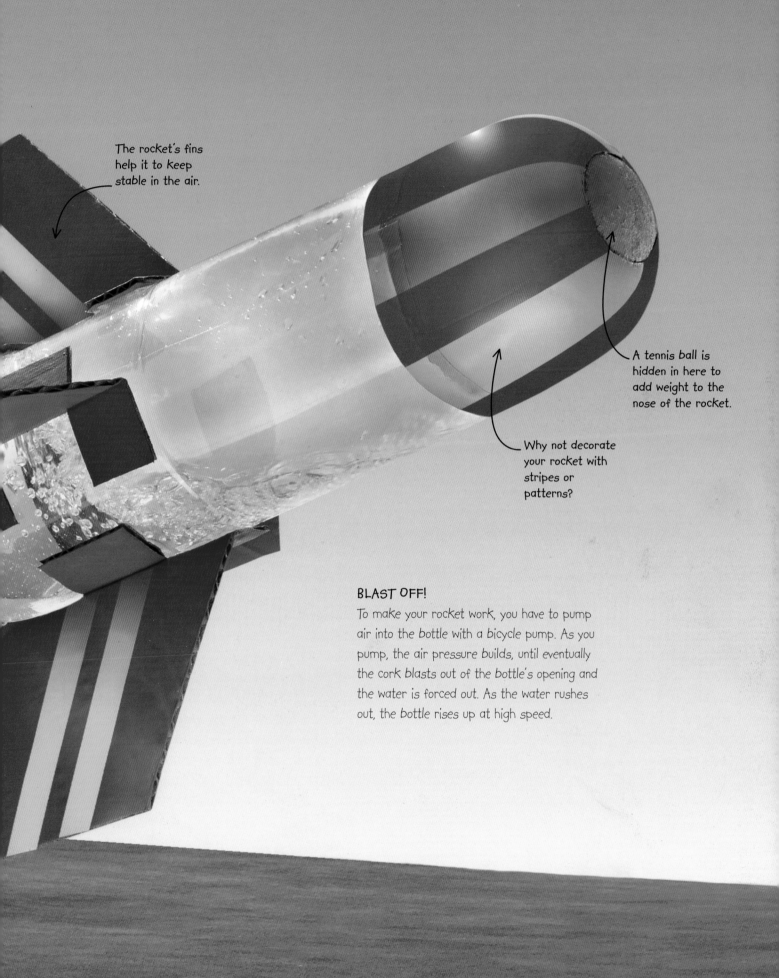

The rocket's fins help it to keep stable in the air.

A tennis ball is hidden in here to add weight to the nose of the rocket.

Why not decorate your rocket with stripes or patterns?

## BLAST OFF!

To make your rocket work, you have to pump air into the bottle with a bicycle pump. As you pump, the air pressure builds, until eventually the cork blasts out of the bottle's opening and the water is forced out. As the water rushes out, the bottle rises up at high speed.

# HOW TO MAKE A
# WATER ROCKET

The sky's the limit with this experiment, which uses air pressure to launch your very own water rocket. Two plastic bottles make the rocket – one for the rocket's body and another to make the nose cone at the top of the rocket. This experiment is a bit tricky, but nobody said rocket science was easy!

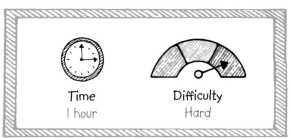

**Time**
1 hour

**Difficulty**
Hard

## WHAT YOU NEED

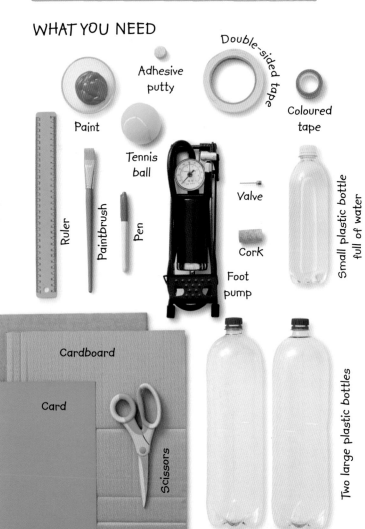

Adhesive putty

Double-sided tape

Paint

Coloured tape

Ruler

Paintbrush

Pen

Tennis ball

Valve

Cork

Foot pump

Small plastic bottle full of water

Cardboard

Card

Scissors

Two large plastic bottles

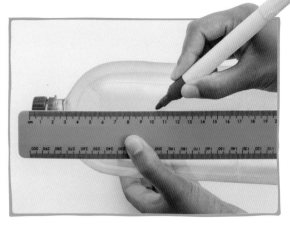

**1** With the pen, make a mark 10 cm (4 in) down from the cap of one plastic bottle.

**2** Wrap the sheet of card around the bottle where you marked it, and draw a straight line around the bottle.

**3** Cut all the way along the line you've drawn. Be careful, and if you have any trouble, ask an adult for help.

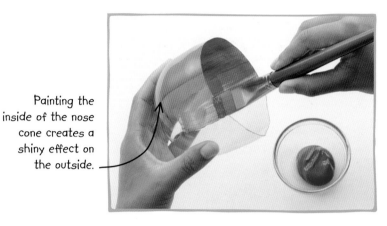

Painting the inside of the nose cone creates a shiny effect on the outside.

**4** Ask an adult to cut off the very top of the bottle, making sure the hole is smaller than the tennis ball.

**5** Paint the inside of the round shape you have made. Your nose cone is nearly complete.

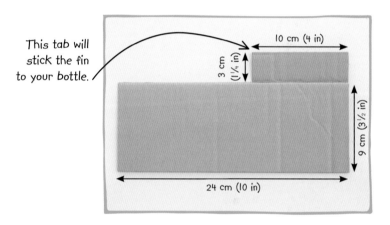

This tab will stick the fin to your bottle.

10 cm (4 in)

3 cm (1¼ in)

9 cm (3½ in)

24 cm (10 in)

**6** Paint the tennis ball. Only part of the ball will show, so you only have to paint half of it.

**7** Draw two rectangles on cardboard, one on top of the other. Make one 10 cm (4 in) long and 3 cm (1¼ in) wide and the other 24 cm (10 in) long and 9 cm (3½ in) wide. Cut along the lines, so you end up with a shape like the one above.

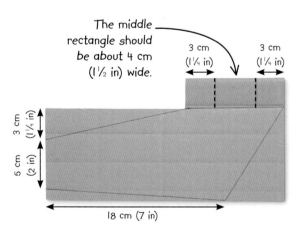

The middle rectangle should be about 4 cm (1½ in) wide.

3 cm (1¼ in)    3 cm (1¼ in)

3 cm (1¼ in)

5 cm (2 in)

18 cm (7 in)

**8** Draw the shape of a fin on the large rectangle, like the one shown here. Draw two dotted lines on the small rectangle, 3 cm (1¼ in) in from each side.

**9** Cut out the fin and then along the dotted lines to create three separate tabs.

You can find a template for the fins at the back of the book.

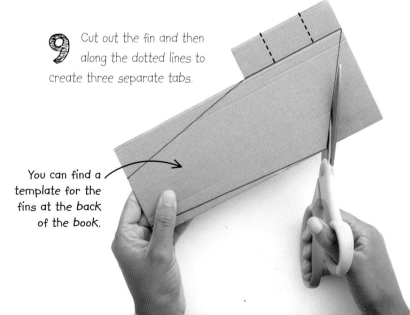

**10** Make three more fins. Use the first one as a template to make sure all your fins are the same shape and size.

**11** Paint all four fins on both sides and leave them to dry. This design is red, but you could decorate your rocket however you like.

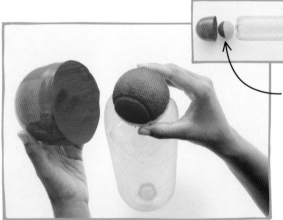

The tennis ball should be placed between the large bottle and the nose cone.

**12** Balance the tennis ball on the flat end of the second large plastic bottle and place the painted end on top, making sure that the ball lines up with the hole in the top.

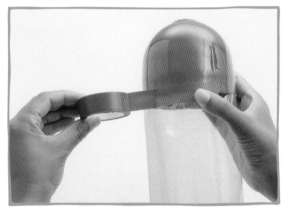

**13** Use coloured tape to secure the nose cone in place. Make sure you attach it firmly – you don't want it to fall off in mid-flight!

Peel off the backing of the double-sided tape.

**14** Fold the fins' top and bottom tabs to the left, and the middle tab to the right. Apply double-sided tape to the underside of each tab.

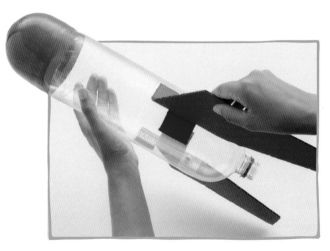

**15** Stick the fins low down on the rocket so that they extend well beyond the neck of the bottle.

The tennis ball in the nose helps to Keep the rocket stable in flight.

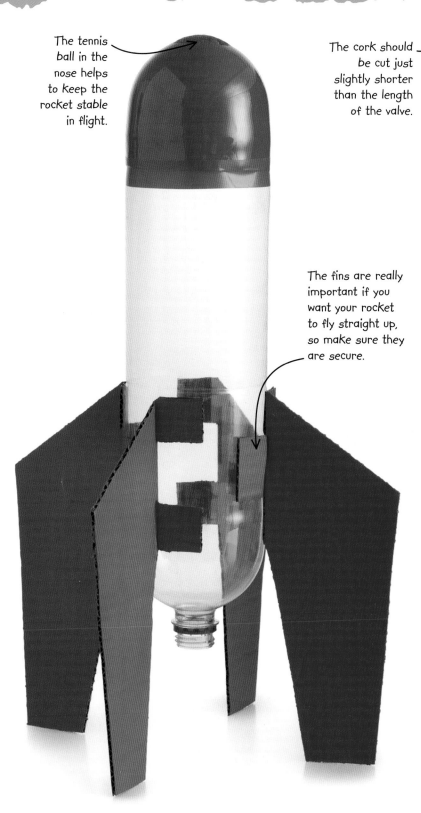

The fins are really important if you want your rocket to fly straight up, so make sure they are secure.

**16** Make sure the bottom of each fin lines up with the others so that the rocket can stand up straight. Your rocket should now look something like this.

The cork should be cut just slightly shorter than the length of the valve.

**17** Check your cork fits in the opening of your bottle, and then ask an adult to help you cut a quarter off at the thinner end.

**18** Push the valve into the middle of the wide end of the cork until it pokes out the other side. Put a piece of adhesive putty on one end, so you don't damage the table.

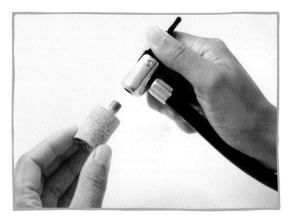

**19** Screw the valve into the foot pump. This is how you'll pump air into the rocket.

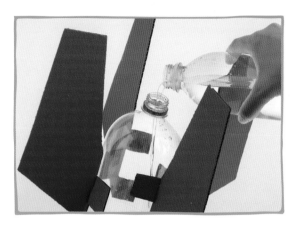

**20** Turn the rocket upside down and use the small bottle to pour in around 500 ml (18 fl oz) of water. Your rocket should be about one-quarter full.

**21** Push the cork firmly into the upturned rocket, being careful not to bend the fins. You are nearly ready for launch!

**22** Stand the rocket on its fins on level ground and, without knocking the bottle over, begin pumping. Keep going until the rocket blasts off.

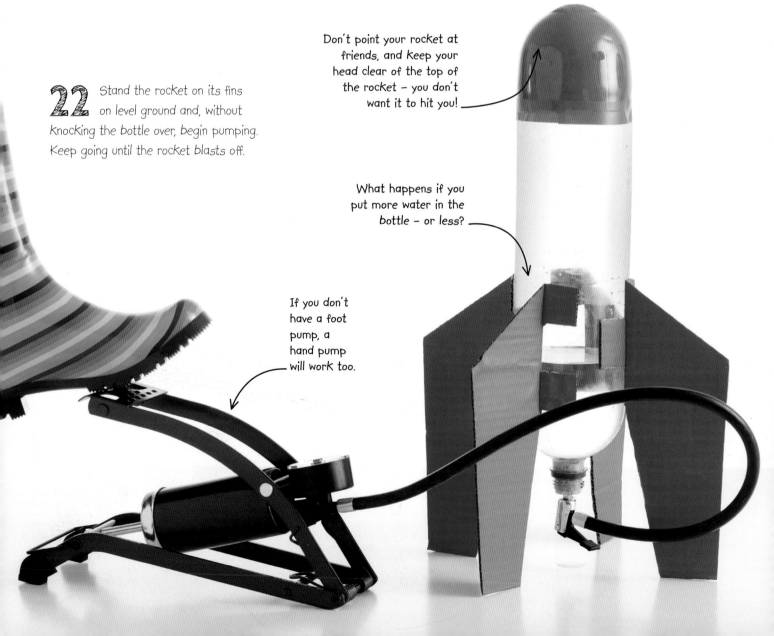

Don't point your rocket at friends, and keep your head clear of the top of the rocket – you don't want it to hit you!

What happens if you put more water in the bottle – or less?

If you don't have a foot pump, a hand pump will work too.

# HOW IT WORKS

Forces always work in pairs. For instance, when you row a boat with a pair of oars, the force of the oars pushing the water creates an opposite force that pushes the oars, and so the boat, forwards. This opposite force, called a reaction force, is what makes rockets fly. When you pump air into your rocket, the air pressure inside builds up until it pushes out the cork and then the water with a powerful force. This downward force creates an upward reaction force that launches the rocket. Once all the water has gone and the pressure inside the bottle is back to normal, the forces disappear and your rocket will fall to Earth.

The reaction force pushes the rocket upwards.

Before you use the pump, the air pressure inside the bottle equals the air pressure outside.

Now that air has been pumped in, the air pressure is now higher inside than out.

The higher pressure pushes the water out.

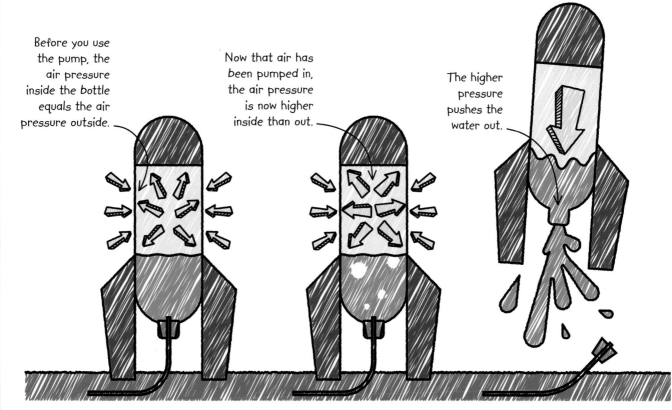

## REAL WORLD SCIENCE
## ROCKET FUEL

A real space rocket works in the same way as your water rocket – but it's not a bicycle pump that increases the pressure inside the rocket. Instead, rocket fuel burns very quickly, producing huge amounts of gas. As new gas is produced, it pushes down on the gas already there, and that pushes the rocket upwards.

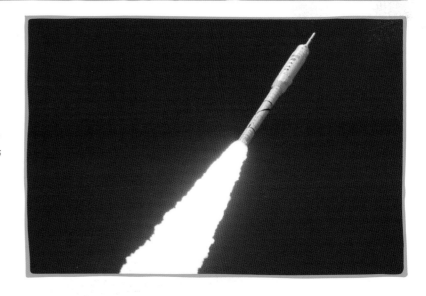

# AIR CANNON

Put the power of moving air in your hands with this amazing air cannon. Pull back the cardboard circle, let go, and the big plastic sheet will snap forwards, sending a burst of air out through a hole in the front. From how far away can you knock over a tower of plastic plant pots, shake the leaves on a tree, or ruffle a friend's hair? Once you've built this design, try thinking of a way to make a much bigger, more powerful air cannon.

This blast is powerful enough to knock over a tower of plastic plant pots!

## THROUGH THE AIR

There's a problem with blasting air across a distance: there's already air in the way! The burst of air fired from the cannon soon loses energy, and slows down – but before it does, it drags in air from all around, passing its energy on to that air. The incoming air creates a vortex ring, an incredible invisible spinning ring of air that moves forwards.

On a really foggy day, you might be able to see the vortex ring moving through the air.

# HOW TO MAKE AN
# AIR CANNON

You'll need really strong tape for this tricky activity because you need to pull quite hard on one part of the cannon. It's also very important to let all the glue dry before you use your air cannon.

**Time**
45 minutes
plus drying time

**Difficulty**
Hard

## WHAT YOU NEED

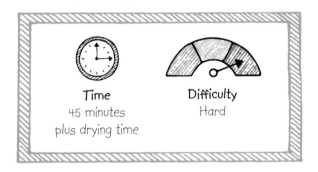

Scissors

White paint    Blue paint    Plastic cup

Pencil

Paintbrush

Strong tape    Rubber band

Glue

Plastic carrier bag

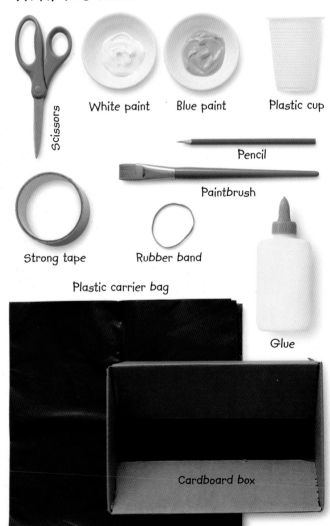

Cardboard box

**1** Carefully cut off all four flaps from the cardboard box. Keep them safe as you'll need them later.

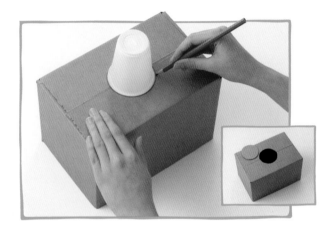

**2** Turn the box upside down and place a plastic cup upside down on the centre of it. Draw around the cup and cut out the circle to make a hole in the box. Ask an adult if you find this tricky.

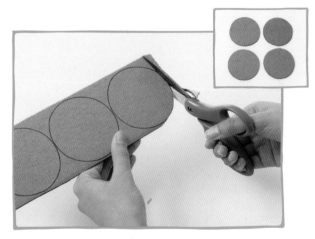

**3** Using the upside-down cup as a template again, cut cardboard circles from the box flaps, so that you have four altogether.

Make sure you leave some excess plastic around the box.

**4** Place the box on the plastic bag and cut around it, leaving a gap of roughly 10 cm (4 in) around the box.

**5** The rubber band will store the energy needed to fire the cannon. Cut it in one place, so that it's no longer a closed circle.

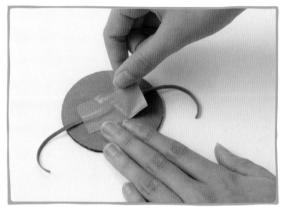

**7** Place the cardboard circle in the middle of the plastic sheet. Stick it down with four pieces of tape.

**6** Stick the rubber band onto the middle of one of the cardboard circles with strong tape. Make sure it is secure, as you'll be pulling on it quite hard.

**8** Glue together the other three cardboard circles to create a stack of circles that you'll use to blast your cannon. Leave it to dry.

**9** Turn over the plastic sheet, and glue the stack of circles you made to the middle, so it's stuck exactly over the cardboard circle that's attached to the other side.

Let the plastic sink into the box.

**10** Stand the box upright with the round hole facing downwards onto the table. Place the plastic sheet – with the cardboard circle facing up – over the top of the box. The sheet should be big enough to sink into the middle of the box.

**11** Seal the edges of the plastic sheet around the top of the box, using strong tape. Make sure the plastic sheet still sinks in the middle.

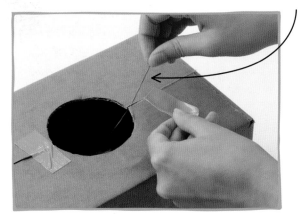

**12** Turn over the box, and reach in through the hole. Pull the ends of the rubber band out, and stick them securely to the outside of the box.

**13** If you like, paint your box with a colourful design, such as the blue-sky pattern shown here. Let the blue paint dry before painting the white clouds.

When you stretch the rubber band, be careful not to snap it.

**14** To make the air cannon work, point it at a target – perhaps some fallen leaves or plastic cups. Pull back the cardboard circle attached to the plastic sheet, then let go! But remember – never point your cannon in people's faces.

When you let go of the handle, the rubber band pulls the plastic sheet forwards quickly, producing a vortex ring.

## HOW IT WORKS

The energy you use to pull on the cardboard circle is stored in the stretched rubber band. When you release the circle, the rubber band releases its energy, pulling the plastic sheet forwards. The plastic sheet's rapid movement passes the energy to the air inside the box, creating a burst of air that is forced out through the hole. This burst of air pushes the stationary air in front of the box out of the way, but, as it passes by, it also drags some along with it, causing the air all around to start spinning in a shape known as a "vortex ring".

Air bursts out of the hole at the front of the air cannon. It's forced out of the box by the plastic sheet's forward movement.

As the air moves forwards, it drags the surrounding air with it. The air starts to spin in the shape of a "vortex ring".

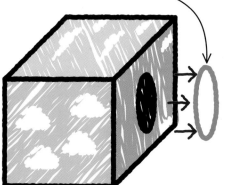
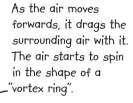
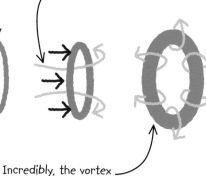

Incredibly, the vortex ring moves through the air long after the original burst of air stopped moving.

## REAL WORLD SCIENCE
### VORTEX RINGS IN NATURE

A fluid is anything that flows – liquids or gases – and vortex rings can happen in any fluid. Sometimes they happen naturally. Occasionally, a volcano with a circular vent (opening) will puff out multiple smoke rings, made of steam and gas. The vortex rings drift upwards because they are produced by rising hot air from within the volcano. Dolphins can also blow out air to create vortex rings underwater, which they chase and try to swim through for fun!

## MAGNETIC FORCES

In this activity, you will make a magnet by magnetizing a pin. Any magnet that can turn around freely will line up so that one end points north and the other end, south. This is because Earth itself is a huge magnet, with one end or "pole" near the North Pole, and another end near the South Pole.

Take your compass needle camping or trekking and you'll always be able to use it to navigate.

# COOL COMPASS

Long before satellite navigation was invented, people relied on compasses to find their way around. A compass has a needle that always points north or south to match up with Earth's magnetic field. You can make your own compass needle using just a dress pin, a plastic cup, and a lid, but you'll need to magnetize the pin for it to work.

As the plastic disc floats on the water, the compass needle can turn freely.

# HOW TO MAKE A
# COOL COMPASS

The most important part of your compass is the compass needle. This activity uses a dress pin, but you could use any thin steel object, such as a needle or the point of a paper clip. The compass needle must be magnetized to make it point north or south, and for that you'll need a magnet.

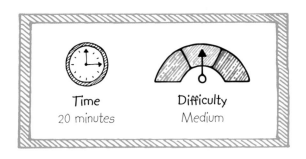

**Time**
20 minutes

**Difficulty**
Medium

## WHAT YOU NEED

Dress pin

Two felt-tip pens

Magnet

Plastic cup

Plastic lid

Adhesive putty

Small bowl of water

Scissors

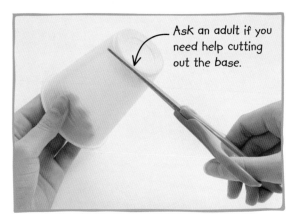

Ask an adult if you need help cutting out the base.

**1** Using the scissors, cut off the base of the plastic cup. This part will float on the water, so that your compass needle can turn freely.

**2** Using a felt-tip pen, draw two dots about 1 cm (½ in) apart, one on either side of the centre of the plastic disc.

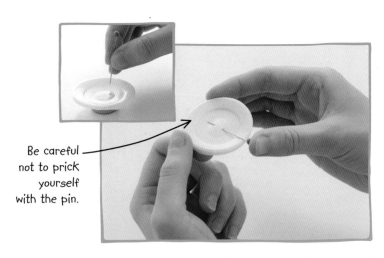

Be careful not to prick yourself with the pin.

**3** Rest the disc on a lump of adhesive putty and poke the pin through each dot. Push the pin down through one hole and up through the other.

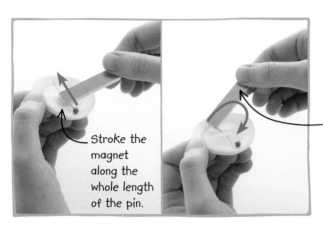

Stroke the magnet along the whole length of the pin.

Make sure you lift the magnet after each stroke.

**4** Now you need to magnetize your pin to make it into a compass needle. Use the magnet to stroke the pin all the way along its length around 40 to 50 times, in one direction only, lifting the magnet away from the end of the pin each time. Always use the same end of the magnet.

**5** Pour water from the bowl into the plastic lid. It doesn't need to be full, but there must be enough water for the disc to float freely.

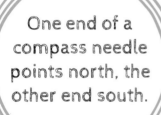

One end of a compass needle points north, the other end south.

Your compass needle will turn around to line up with Earth's magnetic field.

**6** Float the disc on the surface of the water. If your needle doesn't turn, stroke the magnet over it a few more times. It may not yet be magnetized.

**7** Make sure you place your compass away from strong winds, and not right next to electrical appliances or large metal objects.

**7** You can't yet tell if your needle points north or south, so use a smartphone to find north (or ask an adult). Note which end of the pin points north and mark N, E, S, and W on the plastic disc.

**8** Once you have marked the four compass points, you could decorate the plastic disc with a compass rose.

## TAKE IT FURTHER

If you have your magnetized pin, but you don't have the plastic disc, you can *still* use it as a magnetic compass by floating it on a leaf in a puddle – as long as you know whether the point points north or south. In fact, you can use all sort of different materials that float in a puddle, such as cork, polystyrene, or the cap of a plastic bottle. One other thing to try: what happens when you move your magnet close to your floating compass needle?

Your pin will point either north or south. Our pin's point pointed north, but yours might point south.

**9** Your compass is now finished and ready to use. Keep a magnet nearby in case you need to magnetize the needle again.

# HOW IT WORKS

Every magnet has a magnetic field around it and two ends, or "poles", where the field is strongest. Your compass needle is made of steel, which is formed of lots of tiny crystals called domains. Each domain is a tiny magnet, but normally they are jumbled up and their individual magnetic fields cancel each other out. When you stroke the needle, you make all the domains line up, so the magnetic fields point in the same direction.

## UNMAGNETIZED STEEL

The domains (blue arrows) are jumbled up and point in different directions.

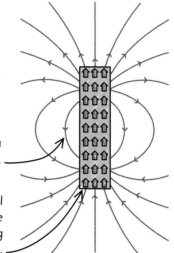

The steel has no magnetic field overall.

The magnetic fields cancel out because the domains are all pointing in different directions.

## MAGNETIZED STEEL

After you stroke the pin with the magnet, the domains (blue arrows) point the same way.

The steel now has a strong magnetic field.

The magnetic fields all add up because the domains are all pointing in the same direction.

## EARTH'S MAGNET

Molten (liquid) iron at Earth's core acts as a strong magnet with a huge magnetic field. Like any magnet, it has two poles – one near the North Pole and one near the South Pole. The two poles of your magnetized pin line up with Earth's magnetic field: the "north-seeking" pole is pulled towards Earth's north magnetic pole, and the "south-seeking pole" is pulled towards the south magnetic pole.

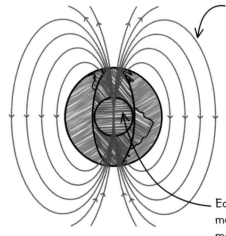

Earth's magnetic field shields us from harmful particles produced by the Sun.

Earth's magnet is made of hot, swirling, molten iron.

# REAL WORLD SCIENCE
## ANIMAL MAGNETIC COMPASS

Many animals have their own magnetic compasses, though not with magnetized metal needles. They have tiny organs that can detect Earth's magnetic field and use it to find their way around. Pigeons use their magnetic super-sense to help them navigate across long distances, and find their way home.

# GORGEOUS GEODES

Sometimes, geologists – scientists who study the solid parts of our planet – are rewarded with beautiful surprises. When they break open rocks, they might find hollow spaces inside, packed with stunning crystals. These rock formations are called geodes, and while real ones take thousands of years to form, you can make yours in just a couple of days!

You could make your egg-shell geodes in loads of different colours.

## COLOURFUL CRYSTALS

Instead of breaking open rocks in the hope of finding a geode, you'll be using an empty egg shell, some food colouring, and a chemical compound called alum to make yours. The alum forms crystals on the surface of the egg shell, and the food colouring will make them bright and colourful.

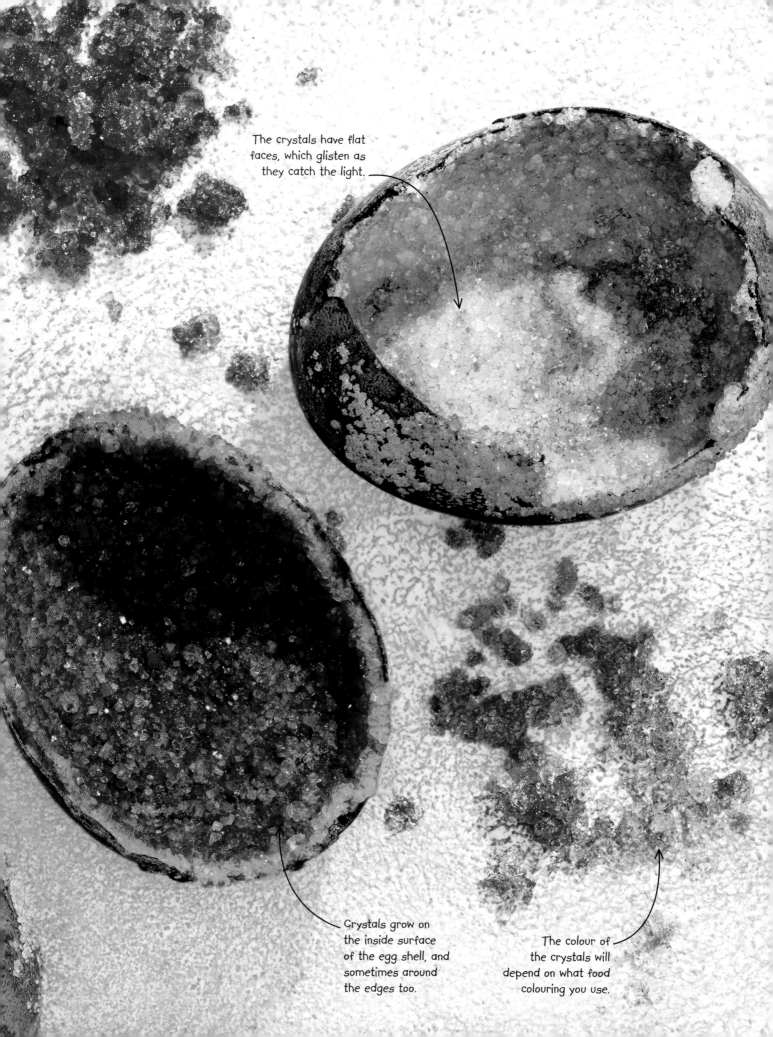

The crystals have flat faces, which glisten as they catch the light.

Crystals grow on the inside surface of the egg shell, and sometimes around the edges too.

The colour of the crystals will depend on what food colouring you use.

# HOW TO CREATE
# GORGEOUS GEODES

The secret ingredient you need to create your own geodes is a chemical compound called alum. You can buy it cheaply at a pharmacy or on the Internet. It's safe to use in small amounts, but don't put any in your mouth, and make sure you wash your hands after handling it.

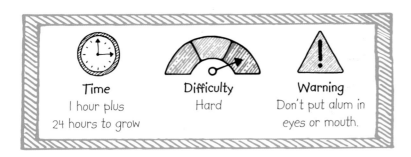

**Time**
1 hour plus
24 hours to grow

**Difficulty**
Hard

**Warning**
Don't put alum in eyes or mouth.

## WHAT YOU NEED

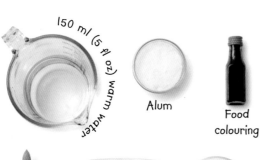
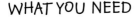

150 ml (5 fl oz) warm water

Alum

Food colouring

Glass bowl

Glue

Plastic cup

Paintbrush

Spoon

Egg

Plate

Paper towel

**1** Before you start, wash your hands. Gently crack the egg against the edge of the bowl and pick away around the crack, to create a hole. You might want to wear protective gloves.

You can keep the inside of the egg for cooking.

**2** Empty the contents of the egg into the bowl. Break a few bits of shell inwards and you should be able to begin to remove the delicate skin, or membrane, that lines the inside of the shell.

Be careful not to break the egg shell.

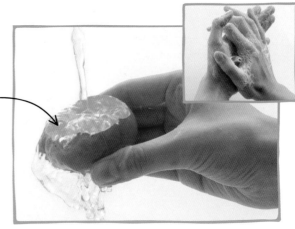

**3** Wash the shell under running water to remove as much of the membrane as possible. Then wash your hands again.

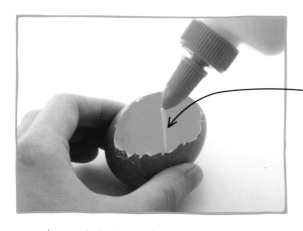

The glue will provide a sticky surface for the alum.

**4** Pour a little bit of glue into the clean, empty egg shell.

**5** Use the paintbrush to spread the glue evenly around the inside of the egg shell.

**6** Use the spoon to sprinkle some alum into the egg shell. Tip out any alum that doesn't stick. You may want to wear gloves for this part, if not, be sure to wash your hands afterwards.

**7** Gradually pour the remaining alum into the warm water and stir with the spoon. Keep adding alum until no more will dissolve, to ensure the solution is really concentrated.

Make sure you stir the mixture to help the alum dissolve.

**8** Add some food colouring – enough to give the the alum solution a deep colour. Stir the mixture again.

**10** Submerge the egg shell in the alum solution. Gently push it down with the spoon to fill the egg shell with solution, being careful not to break it.

**11** Leave the egg shell in the solution for around 24 hours. It will work best somewhere warm and dry. Afterwards, carefully lift it out of the cup.

**9** Pour the alum solution into the plastic cup. The solution should be deep enough for you to submerge the egg shell completely.

When you pour in the solution, some solid alum will be left behind in the jug.

**12** Gently place the egg onto the paper towel.

**13** Take a close look at your egg geode. The alum and the food colouring should have formed lots of small, shiny crystals.

Crystals have grown inside the shell and around the broken edges.

Throw away any remaining alum solution, then wash your hands.

# HOW IT WORKS

When you dissolve the alum in the water, the alum breaks down into tiny parts called ions that mix with the water. The food colouring is already dissolved in water, and that also exists as ions. Every so often, the different ions will meet and may stick together, forming solid crystals. They join in a regular pattern, which is what gives the crystals their distinctive shape.

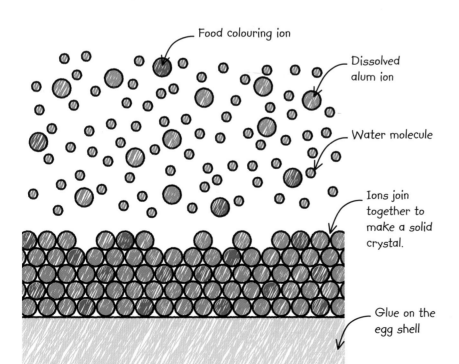

Food colouring ion

Dissolved alum ion

Water molecule

Ions join together to make a solid crystal.

Glue on the egg shell

## REAL WORLD SCIENCE
### REAL GEODES

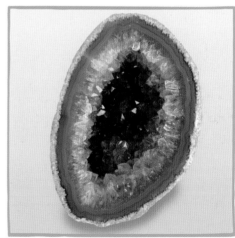

Geodes form inside holes in rock. Often the holes are caused by big bubbles of air in molten lava as it escapes from a volcano. These bubbles become trapped as the lava solidifies into rock. As water seeps through the ground, minerals dissolve in it, and those minerals crystallize inside the holes, creating these beautiful crystals.

To use your latitude locator, you'll have to go out at night and find a locator star or stars. These stars will be different depending on where you are in the world.

# LATITUDE LOCATOR

Early sailors used the stars to figure out exactly where they were on Earth. In the system they created, a location is defined by just two numbers, called latitude and longitude. Your latitude is how far north or south of the equator you are, while your longitude is how far around the planet you are. In this activity you'll make a device that will give your latitude wherever you are in the world.

## WHAT'S YOUR LATITUDE?

Around the middle of planet Earth, at an equal distance from the North Pole and the South Pole, is an imaginary line called the equator. If you live at the equator, your latitude is 0°. If you live at the North Pole, your latitude is 90° north (or +90°), while if you live at the South Pole, it's 90° south (or -90°). Chances are your latitude is somewhere in between. If you go on holiday to somewhere much closer to or further from the equator, you can use your latitude locator to record your new latitude.

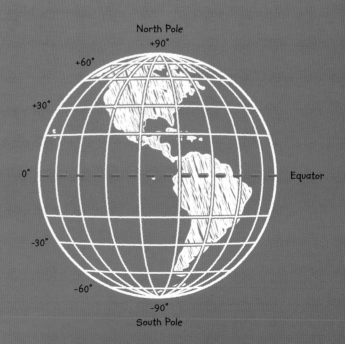

# HOW TO MAKE A
# LATITUDE LOCATOR

It's really easy to make this latitude locator. First, turn to the *back* of this *book* to find the template for the scale you'll need. Trace the template onto a sheet of paper (or photocopy it) and cut it out. Then it just takes a bit more cutting and sticking.

**Time**
30 minutes

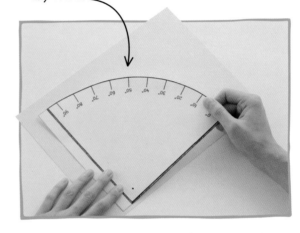

**Difficulty**
Medium

## WHAT YOU NEED

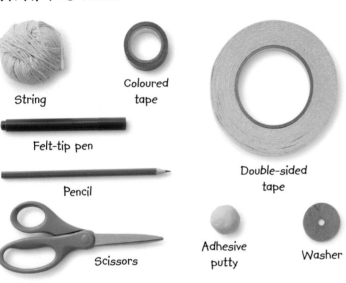

String

Coloured tape

Felt-tip pen

Pencil

Double-sided tape

Scissors

Adhesive putty

Washer

A4 sheet of card

A4 sheet of paper

A4 sheet of card

The piece of card you use can be any colour.

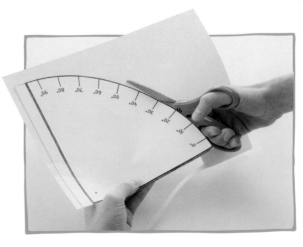

**1** Stick several pieces of double-sided tape to the back of the paper. Peel off the protective strips, and stick down onto a piece of card.

**2** Carefully cut the card around the edge of the paper with a pair of scissors. Remember to recycle any leftover pieces of card.

The putty makes it easier to push the pencil through the paper.

**3** Put a piece of adhesive putty underneath the dot in the corner of your scale. Then use the sharp end of the pencil to make a small hole.

**4** Cut a 20 cm (8 in) length of string. Thread one end through the hole and tie a double knot, near the end of the string at the back of the card.

Latitude affects how many hours of sunlight a location gets each day.

**5** Roll the other piece of card tightly around the felt-tip pen, to make a narrow tube. This will be your sighting tube, which you will look through when measuring your latitude.

Make sure the card is wrapped tightly around the felt-tip pen to stop it from unravelling.

**6** Use one side of a piece of double-sided tape to stick the card tube closed. Hold an end up to your eye to check you can see through it.

**7** Peel off the protective strip from the double-sided tape. This will let you stick the sighting tube to the latitude scale in the next step.

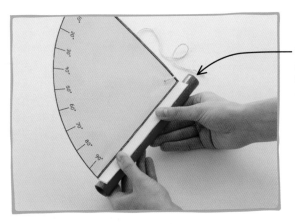

Be careful not to squash the tube when you attach the scale.

**8** Find the tab along the edge of the latitude scale, fold it, and press it firmly against the double-sided tape running along the sighting tube.

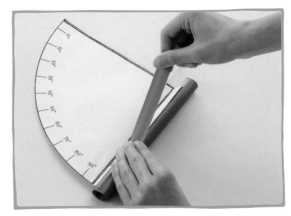

**9** Use a length of coloured tape to stick down the tab of the latitude scale to the sighting tube. This will firmly secure the scale to the tube.

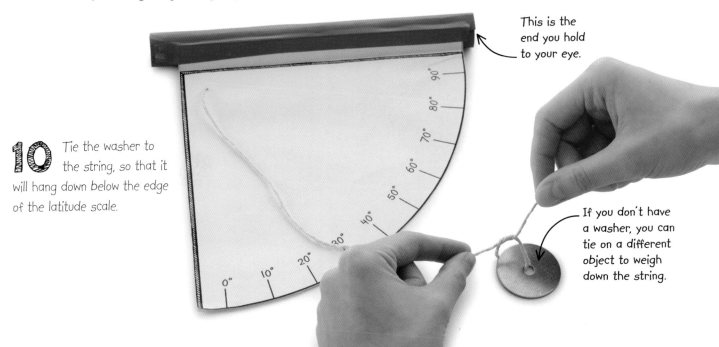

This is the end you hold to your eye.

**10** Tie the washer to the string, so that it will hang down below the edge of the latitude scale.

If you don't have a washer, you can tie on a different object to weigh down the string.

# HOW TO USE IT

To use the latitude locator, go outside with an adult on a clear night, preferably to an open space away from street lighting. You then need to find a point in the sky. This point will be the North Celestial Pole if you are in the Northern Hemisphere, or the South Celestial Pole if you are in the Southern Hemisphere. To find these points, use the directions given below - it will really help if you have a compass to find north or south. Look at that point in the sky through your sighting tube and make sure the washer is hanging freely. Your latitude is the angle shown at the point where the string crosses the scale.

## NORTH CELESTIAL POLE

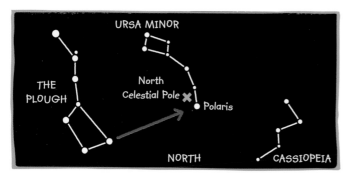

If you live in the Northern Hemisphere, stand facing north, look up, and find the bright constellation known as the Plough. Follow the line made by edge of the front of the Plough to find the star Polaris - which is close to the North Celestial Pole.

## SOUTH CELESTIAL POLE

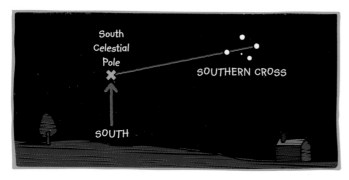

If you live in the Southern Hemisphere, there is no bright star close to the South Celestial Pole. Instead, you need to locate a group of stars called the Southern Cross. Follow an imaginary line from the two stars that are furthest apart. Where that line crosses another imaginary line coming up from the horizon at due south is where you need to point your latitude locator.

# HOW IT WORKS

Gravity is a force that pulls everything on Earth downwards towards the centre of the planet. As a result, your latitude locator's washer makes the string hang vertically down. If you live at the equator, whether you are looking at the North or South Celestial Pole, you will be looking at the horizon - and you will read your latitude as 0°. If you are at one of the Poles, you will have to look directly above your head to see the Celestial Pole, and so your string will show your latitude as 90° north or south. Your home is probably somewhere in between these extremes.

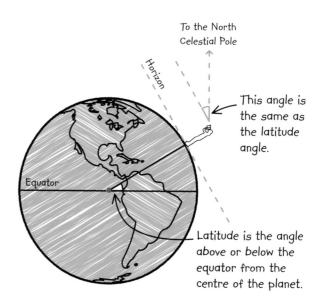

## REAL WORLD SCIENCE
### NAVIGATING AT SEA

Before satellite navigation, sailors would find their latitude using a sextant, a clever device that measures angles between objects. The sextant is still used today, and it can also help sailors to work out their longitude, so they have a really good idea of exactly where they are in the world.

# PAPER SUNDIAL

As the Sun moves across the sky during the day, the shadows cast by objects move too. With a sundial, you can use these shadows to tell the time. It's easy to make your own sundial using a drinking straw and a piece of paper, but you'll only be able to use it between spring and autumn. During winter, the Sun is too low in the sky for the straw to cast a shadow on the paper.

The Sun will soon set, in the west.

## READING THE SUNDIAL

You may have to adjust the time the sundial shows for daylight saving time, a period when clocks are changed to give more daylight in the evening. Ask an adult if and when that applies to your location. When it does, you'll usually have to add an hour to the time shown on the sundial.

This sundial shows the time is about half-past four in the afternoon.

6 P.M.     6 A.M.

# HOW TO MAKE A
# PAPER SUNDIAL

First you'll need to trace or photocopy one of the templates at the back of this book. There is one template for use in the Northern Hemisphere and another for the Southern Hemisphere. Make sure you use the correct version. If you don't know which hemisphere you live in, ask an adult. You'll also need to find out a number called your latitude: you can ask an adult, look online, or make your own latitude locator to find out – see pages 144–149!

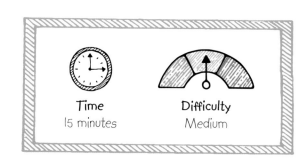

**Time**
15 minutes

**Difficulty**
Medium

## WHAT YOU NEED

Plastic straw

Pencil

Adhesive putty

Scissors

Coloured tape

Cardboard

A4 sheet of paper

Ruler

Compass

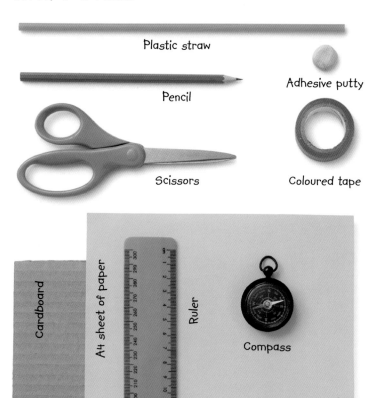

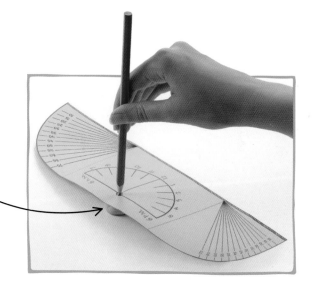

The adhesive putty helps to protect the work surface.

**1** Make sure you have a copy of the right template. Cut it out and put some adhesive putty under where the dot is at the top of the hour scale. Make a hole with the pencil through the dot.

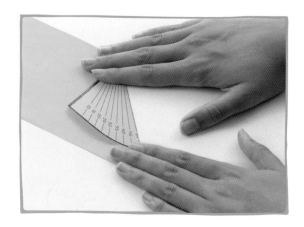

**2** Find your angle of latitude along the scale at the side of the paper. Fold and crease along that angle (50° latitude in the example).

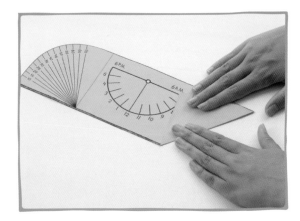

**3** Turn the template over and fold again along the crease you created. Repeat steps 2 and 3 for the scale on the other side of the template.

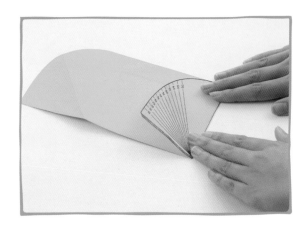

**4** Now unfold the angled sides, then fold and crease along the dotted straight lines on either side of the sundial's main panel.

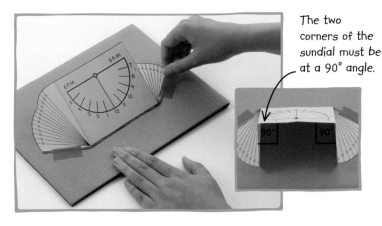

The two corners of the sundial must be at a 90° angle.

**5** Using tape, attach the creased sundial template to the piece of cardboard. Make sure the sides of the sundial are vertical.

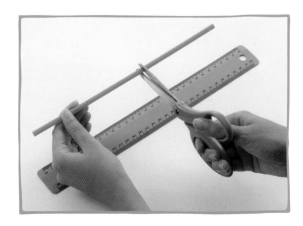

**6** Cut a piece of the straw about 15 cm (6 in) long. This will be the "gnomon" – the piece of the sundial casting the shadow that tells the time.

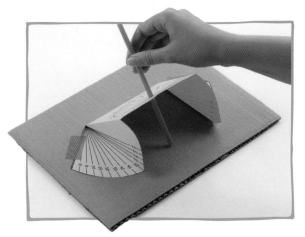

**7** Carefully push the straw through the hole in the sundial's face, from the top down to the cardboard. Ensure it's at right angles to the face.

Keeping the paper and straw in the right place can be fiddly – if you get stuck ask an adult for help.

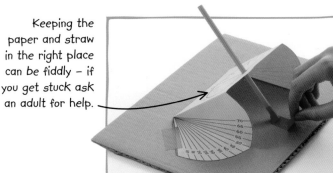

**8** Secure the straw to the cardboard base, making sure that the sundial's face remains flat and that the straw is still at right angles to it.

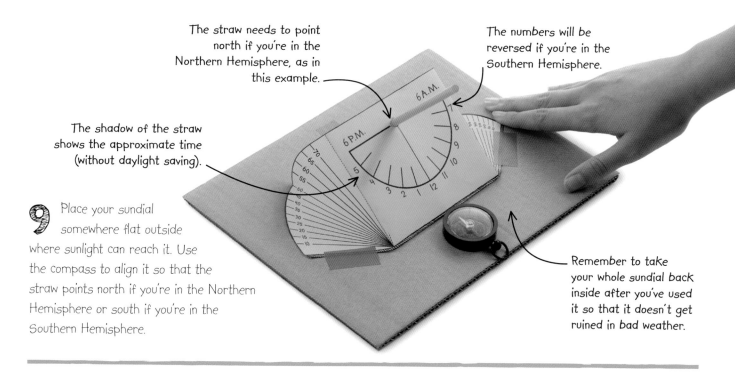

The straw needs to point north if you're in the Northern Hemisphere, as in this example.

The numbers will be reversed if you're in the Southern Hemisphere.

The shadow of the straw shows the approximate time (without daylight saving).

**9** Place your sundial somewhere flat outside where sunlight can reach it. Use the compass to align it so that the straw points north if you're in the Northern Hemisphere or south if you're in the Southern Hemisphere.

Remember to take your whole sundial back inside after you've used it so that it doesn't get ruined in bad weather.

# HOW IT WORKS

Planet Earth is spinning, and as a result, the Sun appears to move across our sky. It rises in the east, at noon it reaches its highest point, and then sets in the west. Earth takes 24 hours to make one complete rotation (360°) – so it turns 15° per hour, and the shadows created by the Sun shift by 15° per hour. The lines on the sundial are spaced 15° apart, so the space between each line represents one hour.

## REAL WORLD SCIENCE
## SHADOWS

Your own shadow is very long just after sunrise and just before sunset, when the Sun is low in the sky. Your shadow is shortest at noon. If you stood at the equator at noon on midsummer's day, you would have no shadow at all, because the Sun would be directly overhead.

## NORTHERN HEMISPHERE

The Sun moves 15° across the sky each hour.

In the Northern Hemisphere, the Sun is to the South.

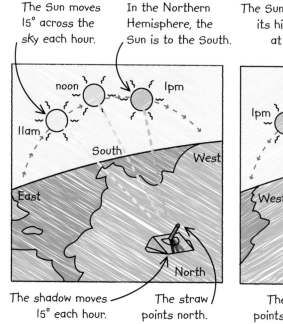

The shadow moves 15° each hour.

The straw points north.

## SOUTHERN HEMISPHERE

The Sun is at its highest at noon.

In the Southern Hemisphere, the Sun is to the North.

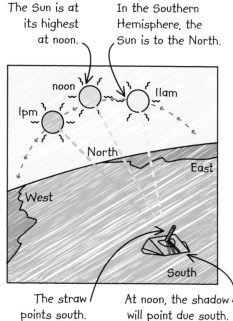

The straw points south.

At noon, the shadow will point due south.

# TEMPLATES

These are the templates you need for the anemometer, twirling helicopter, water rocket, latitude locator, and sundial. You can either trace the lines onto a piece of paper or photocopy the page you need. For the sundial, make sure you use the correct template - one is designed for use in the Northern Hemisphere, and the other is designed for use in the Southern Hemisphere.

Anemometer p.58

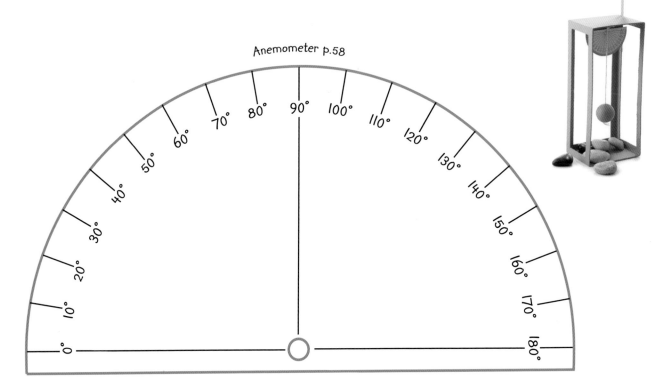

Twirling helicopter p.106

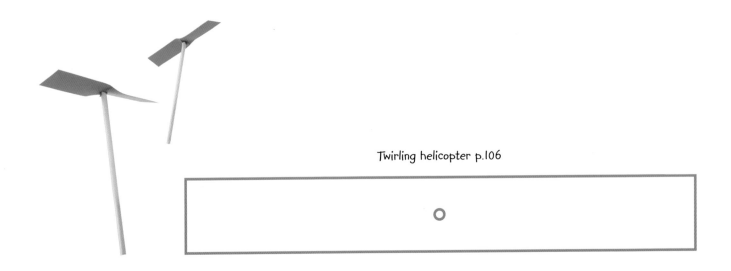

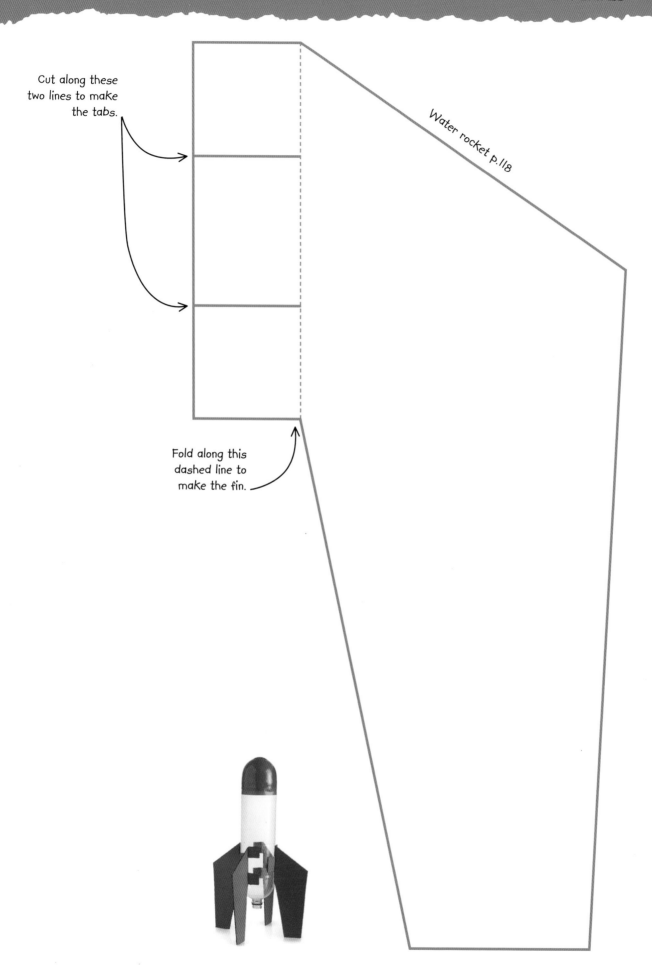

Cut along these two lines to make the tabs.

Water rocket p.118

Fold along this dashed line to make the fin.

Latitude locator p.144

Fold along this dashed
line to make a tab that
will attach the locator to
the viewing rod.

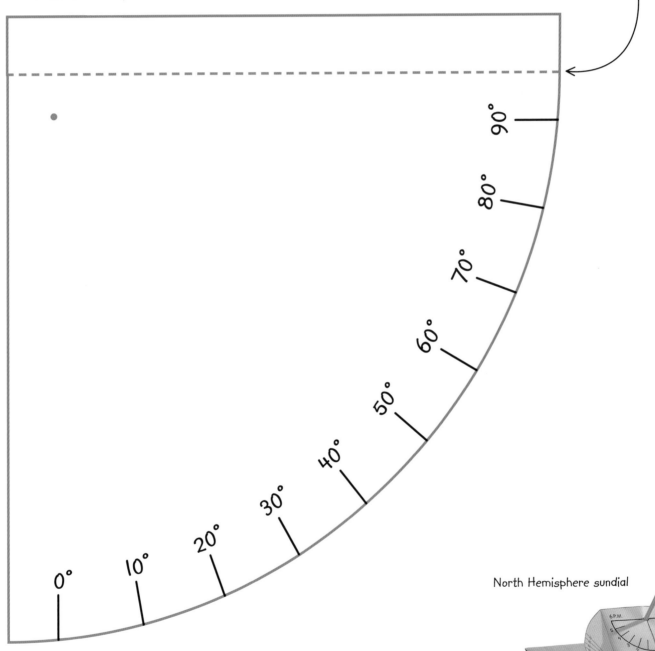

90°

80°

70°

60°

50°

40°

30°

20°

10°

0°

North Hemisphere sundial

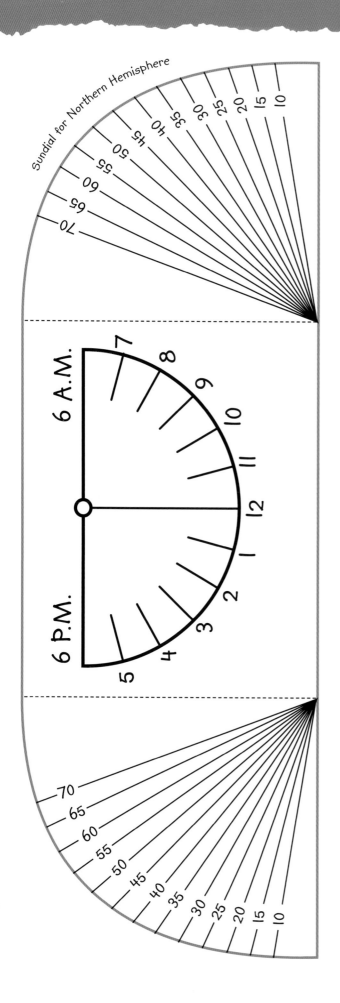

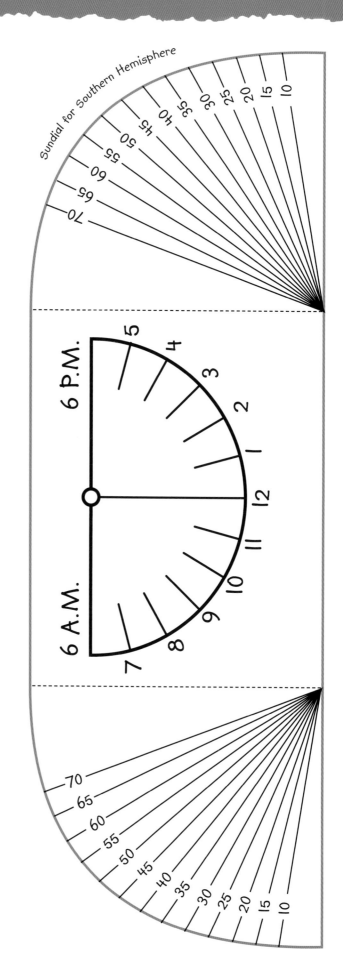

# GLOSSARY

## ANEMOMETER

A device meteorologists use to measure wind speed, normally in kilometres per hour or miles per hour.

## ATMOSPHERIC PRESSURE

The pressure of the air around you, caused by the weight of the layer of air around our planet called the atmosphere.

## BACTERIA

Tiny living things too small to be seen without a microscope. Some bacteria are useful – for example in cheese making – but others can cause disease or cause food to go bad.

## BAROMETER

A device meteorologists use to measure atmospheric pressure.

## CALIBRATION

Putting numbers on the scale of a measuring device such as a barometer, so that you can take actual readings, instead of just "higher and lower".

## CAMOUFLAGE

Colours or patterns that match an object's surroundings, making it harder to see. Many animals have camouflaged fur or skin to hide from predators.

## CELL

The smallest part of a living thing that is alive. All living things are made of cells. Some, such as bacteria, are just single cells, while a tree is made of trillions of cells, and so are you.

## CELLULOSE

A substance produced by plants that forms their cell walls and strengthens the tiny tubes that carry water up the stem and into leaves.

## COLLOID

If two chemicals mix well but don't properly dissolve, they form a colloid. Colloids usually consist of tiny droplets or bubbles of one chemical dispersed in another.

## COMPOUND

A substance containing chemically combined atoms of two or more different elements.

## CONTRACTION

Getting shorter. Muscles work by contracting – in fact they can only contract.

## CRYSTAL

A solid with a regular shape, often with flat faces and straight edges, such as a diamond. Crystals have regular shapes because their atoms are arranged in a repeating pattern.

## CYLINDER

A three-dimensional shape that has a circle as a cross-section. A cardboard tube is a cylinder.

## DENSITY

A measure of how much mass (stuff) is present in a certain volume. Rock is much more dense than water, for example.

## DOMAIN

A small part of a magnetic material, such as iron. Each domain has its own magnetic field, and when the material is magnetized, the domains' fields all line up.

## EQUATOR

An imaginary line around the middle of Earth, halfway between the North Pole and the South Pole.

## EROSION

Wearing away. Rocks and soil can be eroded by wind and rain.

## FORCE

A push or a pull. Forces change the way objects move, making them speed up, slow down, or change direction. They can also change the shape of an object.

## FUNGUS

A type of living thing, neither a plant nor an animal, that feeds off rotting matter, such as dead wood. Mushrooms are the part of a fungus that grows above ground.

## GEOLOGY

The scientific study of solid parts of Earth, such as rocks, soil, and mountains, and how they form.

## GRAVITY

The force that keeps you on the ground. Gravity pulls everything down, towards the centre of our planet, and gives things weight.

## HABITAT

Where living things live.

## HEMISPHERE

One half of a sphere. In particular, it is used to describe the half of our planet above or below the equator.

## HUMIDITY

A measure of how much water vapour is in the air. When the humidity is high, there is a good chance of rain or fog.

## HYDROPHILIC

Means "water-loving", and describes one end of a soap molecule that is pulled to water molecules.

## HYDROPHOBIC

Means "water-hating", and describes one end of a soap molecule that is pushed away from water molecules.

## HYDROPONICS

Growing plants without soil. Plants grown hydroponically get all the nutrients they need from their water supply. A plant would normally find these nutrients in the soil.

## IMMISCIBLE

Means "un-mixable", and describes two liquids that will not mix, such as oil and vinegar.

## ISOBAR

A line on a weather map that joins up all the places where the atmospheric pressure is the same.

## LATITUDE

A measure of how far north or south of the equator you are. The latitude of the equator is 0°, while the North Pole has a latitude of +90° and the South Pole, -90°.

## MAGNETIC FIELD

The region around a magnet, in which another magnet or a magnetic material will experience a force.

## MASS

A measure of the amount of matter (stuff) in an object.

## METEOROLOGIST

A scientist who studies the weather, such as a weather forecaster.

## MOLECULE

A tiny particle of matter, made up of two or more atoms joined together. All water molecules are made of two hydrogen atoms joined to an oxygen atom, for example ($H_2O$). All molecules of a particular substance are identical.

## MUCUS

A slimy solution produced by living things, made from water and other substances. In your body, mucus helps food slide through your digestive system and catches bacteria in your nose, which stops them getting to your lungs.

## MULCH

Dead leaves and other plant matter that is laid on top of soil where plants are growing, to help protect the soil.

## MYCELIUM

The main part of a fungus, made of fine threads that are often hidden from view. Mushrooms grow out of mycelium hidden in the ground.

## PRESSURE

The force of air or water pushing on things. Air pressure falls as you climb a mountain, and water pressure rises as you dive deeper in the sea.

## PROBOSCIS

A tube through which butterflies and other insects suck in their food. A proboscis can also be a snout or a trunk on mammals such as elephants.

## RECYCLE

To make something new from the materials of something that is no longer needed. Plastic and metal are often melted down, so they can be made into new items.

## ROTOR

The spinning part of a helicopter, which produces an upward force called lift as it moves through the air.

## SOAP FILM

The thin layer of soapy water that forms the outside of a soap bubble.

## SOLUTION

A substance broken down into individual molecules or atoms and thoroughly mixed in with the molecules of a liquid – as happens when sugar dissolves in water.

## SOLVENT

A liquid that dissolves things easily, to form solutions. Often the word refers to liquids that evaporate quickly into the air, leaving behind whatever was dissolved in it.

## SPHERICAL

Round like a ball. A sphere is a three-dimensional object.

## VOLUME

The amount of space something takes up, normally measured in millilitres, litres, or cubic metres.

## VORTEX

A region of a liquid or gas that is spinning, such as the swirling water that forms when water drains through a plughole. You form invisible vortices every time you move through the air.

## WATER VAPOUR

When water evaporates it forms an invisible gas in the air, called water vapour.

## WEIGHT

The downward force on an object caused by gravity. The more mass something has, the more it weighs.

# INDEX

## ACKNOWLEDGMENTS

The publisher would like to thank the following people for their assistance in the preparation of this book:
NandKishor Acharya, Alex Lloyd, Syed MD Farhan, Pankaj Sharma, and SmjiIka Surla for design assistance; Sam AtKinson, Ben Ffrancon Davies, Sarah MacLeod, and Sophie Parkes for editorial assistance; Steve Crozier for picture retouching; Sean Ross for additional illustrations; Jemma Westing for making and testing experiments; Helen Peters for indexing; Victoria Pyke for proofreading; Caleb Gilbert, Hayden Gilbert, Molly Greenfield, Nadine King, Kit Lane, Helen Leech, Sophie Parkes, Rosie Peet, and Abi Wright for modelling.

The publisher would like to thank the following for their Kind permission to reproduce their photographs:
(Key: a-above; b-below/bottom; c-centre; f-far; l-left; r-right; t-top)

15 Alamy Stock Photo: Prime Ministers Office (br) 19 naturepl.com: Adrian Davies (br) 25 Alamy Stock Photo: Jeff Gynane (tr). 31 Alamy Stock Photo: Science History Images (bl) 35 Getty Images: Mmdi (crb). 39 Getty Images: Bloomberg (crb). 43 Alamy Stock Photo: Mira (bl) 49 123RF.com: Adrian Hillman (bl). 53 Alamy Stock Photo: Joel Douillet (bl) 57 Alamy Stock Photo: YAY Media AS (bc) 65 Depositphotos Inc: flypix (bl). 71 123RF.com: bjul (crb) 79 Alamy Stock Photo: Nature

Photographers Ltd (br). 85 Alamy Stock Photo: RGB Ventures / SuperStock (t). 89 NASA: (crb) 91 Anatoly Beloshchin: (crb). 99 Dreamstime.com: Maria Medvedeva (cr). 103 Alamy Stock Photo: NOAA (bc). 109 123RF.com: aleksanderdn (crb). 117 123RF.com: epicstockmedia (bl) 125 Alamy Stock Photo: Newscom (br). 131 Ardea: Augusto Leandro Stanzani (br). 137 123RF.com: Dmitry Maslov (bl). 143 Alamy Stock Photo: Dafinchi (bl). 149 Alamy Stock Photo: Dino Fracchia (crb). 153 Alamy Stock Photo: Sergio Azenha (crb)

All other images © Dorling Kindersley
For further information see: www.dkimages.com